Helping People Learn

Dr Jake Reynolds

Jake Reynolds is a Director of the University of Cambridge Programme for Industry (CPI), the University's centre of excellence in work-based, workplace learning. He designs and directs educational programmes that promote learning, leadership and change in organisations, many of which are supported by innovative partnerships, learning processes and electronic media. Jake has a DPhil from the University of Oxford.

The Chartered Institute of Personnel and Development is the leading publisher of books and reports for personnel and training professionals, students, and all those concerned with the effective management of people at work.
For full details of all our titles, please contact the Publishing Department:

Tel.: 020 8263 3387
Fax: 020 8263 3850
E-mail: publish@cipd.co.uk

The catalogue of all CIPD titles can be viewed on the CIPD website: www.cipd.co.uk/bookstore

For details of CIPD research projects:
www.cipd.co.uk/research

Helping People Learn

Strategies for moving from training to learning

Dr Jake Reynolds

Cambridge Programme for Industry

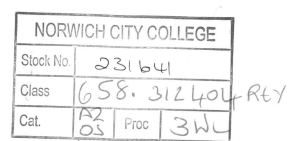

First published 2004
Reprinted 2007

Cover design by Curve
Designed by Beacon GDT
Typeset by Paperweight
Printed in Great Britain by Short Run Press, Exeter

British Library Cataloguing in Publication Data:
A catalogue record for this book is available from the British Library

ISBN 978 1 84398 105 3

Chartered Institute of Personnel and Development
151 The Broadway, Wimbledon, London SW19 1JQ

Tel.: 020 8971 9000
Fax: 020 8263 3333
E-mail: www.cipd.co.uk

incorporated by Royal Charter: Registered charity no. 1079797.

Contents

Acknowledgements

The CIPD would like to thank the following people for providing valuable insights and comments during the preparation of this report: Roger Bellis, Andy Cooke, Peter Honey, Robin Mason, Stuart Reid and all the members of the CIPD's Learning, Training and Development Vice-President's Panel. Thanks also to Polly Courtice for describing the conditions necessary to promote learning in organisations as a 'growth medium'.

The CIPD would also like to express its thanks to the many members who offered their ideas at all stages of the research. Our particular gratitude to the following organisations that convened meetings to discuss the *Helping People Learn* project: Rolls-Royce, Marks and Spencer, the CMPS and Linklaters.

Foreword

One useful indicator of the mood of human resource development comes from the responses to questions in the CIPD Annual Training and Development Survey. In the 2004 survey, respondents were presented with a series of statements on organisational approaches to learning and development; they were asked to indicate the extent of their agreement with these statements. The one that commanded the widest support (at 97.7 per cent agreement) was 'people learn in all manner of ways, including training'. No surprises here: indeed the only question is what was going through the minds of the 2.3 per cent of respondents who demurred.

The next three statements in terms of support, taken together, could, however, be said to describe the new orthodoxy for training in organisations. They were: 'Individuals need advice and support if they are to take more responsibility for their own learning', 'Line managers should play a significant role in helping their teams to learn and develop', 'Employees need to take more responsibility for their own learning and development.' These statements transmit a clear view that a shift in approach from training (interventions designed to teach employees new knowledge and skills) to learning (an ongoing process which lies in the domain of the individual) is not something that just happens. It is not enough, to return to some embarrassing recent history for the profession, to make generic e-learning material available to the learner through the corporate intranet and hope that somebody will learn something useful. A proactive approach that recognises the objectives and operating reality of the organisation is required: in short, it is necessary to create, implement and monitor a learning strategy.

In developing such a strategy the modern human resource development professional must consider a wide range of questions. These 'how to' questions involve the following (and more): ensuring that learning is aligned with appropriate corporate objectives; developing awareness of the value of relevant learning to the organisation; promoting learner confidence and ability; creating processes so that the learner has the time and freedom to learn. These activities and conditions do not arise as a result of a top-down diktat. It is not simply a matter of the chief executive stating that he or she sees people as the most important asset and intends to introduce a learning organisation (whatever that might be). Creating the circumstances in which employees wish to acquire the skills and knowledge that enable them to be more effective in their job is a dispersed activity. It demands the attention of the full range of managers and employees throughout the organisation.

In keeping with the times, the 2004 Annual Training and Development Survey contained a specific section on 'Helping people learn.' It asked respondents to indicate those activities felt to be the most important in helping employees to learn effectively at work. The one that commanded most support was 'ensuring that the organisational culture is supportive of learning and development'. That is easier said than done. Not only is cultural change a dispersed activity, it is heavily dependent on the context of the organisation and its business objectives. What is appropriate in a knowledge-intensive software house would be very different from the intervention and support activities needed in an engineering works. The public sector and not-for-profit voluntary organisation will produce a different set of challenges. There are no 'tips and tricks' that can be read across from elsewhere; it is a job for the competent HRD manager to work through in his or her own organisation.

The starting point, however, must be to consider any actions or interventions against the background of learning in the modern organisation. Here is where the contribution of the Cambridge Programme for Industry is of immense value. In this report, and its predecessor, *How do People Learn?*, Jake Reynolds and his colleagues have analysed learning theory, synthesised the complex and sometimes arcane discussions and expressed their conclusions in a way that will resonate with the thinking professional. The last chapter on 'Learning interventions', for example, which articulates some new roles for the function, will strike a chord with many readers. Some may justifiably say they have adopted such approaches already, and indeed their responses to an earlier discussion document have shaped many of the arguments that Jake Reynolds has advanced. Neither, as will be evident, need any trainer (to use the traditional term) be threatened by the emerging new orthodoxy that is set out in this final chapter. Many more opportunities beckon than there are threats: the challenge is to use existing knowledge and skills in a new way.

Hopefully, *Helping People Learn* will assist our members to meet these challenges. We shall be continuing and extending this important strand of CIPD work over the course of the next year by offering guidance on practical implementation in organisations. The website www.cipd.co.uk/ helpingpeoplelearn will contain details of these initiatives. Immediately, we hope that this Report will make a useful contribution towards creating the conditions for effective learning in organisations.

Martyn Sloman

CIPD Adviser, Learning, Training and Development
June 2004

Why this report?

How can learning be supported, accelerated and directed towards an organisation's strategic needs? This has become a key business question for organisations today. The answer is complex. Many factors are influential, ranging from broad features like the vision and values of the organisation, to specific features like the degree of support for learning provided by managers.

As its title suggests, this Report focuses on the enabling conditions for effective learning in organisations – the conditions in which employees find themselves working on a routine basis, not just when they attend training courses. The need to enable learning among employees, rather than deliver or direct it, is a recurrent theme of the Report. The consequences of this shift will be explored in later sections.

This Report builds on the 2002 Research Report *How do People Learn?* and the Change Agenda *Focus on the Learner*, published in the following year.

In preparing this Report we were able to call on the expertise of a large number of CIPD members who contributed to the research by submitting comments at conferences and local meetings or by sending their ideas and case illustrations via the special website. The quotations contained in this Research Report have been drawn from these submissions.

Ultimately, action can only be taken by those who are working in, or advising, organisations that are willing to make a commitment to individual and team learning. At the end of each chapter we have set out a series of questions to assist them in developing their plans and ideas. It is their actions that will translate theory and concepts into practice.

Executive summary

The capacity to adapt is the greatest gift of learning. It allows the learner to remain agile in the face of uncertain future conditions, whereas other outcomes of learning, such as new knowledge and skills, tend to have specific applications and a shorter shelf-life. The challenge for HRD professionals is to move from a strategy based upon delivery of training to one based upon support for learning. But how can we create organisations that enable employees to assert control over their learning rather than remain dependent on external support? Such organisations would surely be better equipped to meet the future business challenges.

In this Report we address this question in two ways. Firstly, we explore the climate for learning in organisations. In the right climate, we propose that employees will commit their energies to the vision of the organisation, speeding up the process of improvement and innovation. This is an area where managers have considerable sway over learning. The organisation depends upon their 'learning leadership' skills.

While it is very important for people to commit to the organisations they work for, and to want to seek to improve it, commitment alone does not guarantee that learning will be timely, productive or systematic. Moreover, it cannot guarantee that individuals will share their learning effectively in groups or apply it to the wider challenge of organisational change. Many factors intervene between the commitment to learn and the impact of learning in practice: the quality of individual learning skills; the effectiveness of group behaviour; and the degree to which the culture of the organisation is open to adaptation.

Secondly, then, we explore the issue of learning capabilities ('learning how to learn'), at individual,

group and organisational levels. We suggest that learning capabilities bring insight and discipline to the process of learning, helping employees (and the groups in which they operate) to draw on their experience, work effectively with others and increase their strategic contribution. The presence of generic learning skills helps an organisation to remain flexible in the face of unpredictable future conditions. Yet their importance is under-recognised at present by organisations, even by HRD professionals. How much effort did your training and development function expend on developing learning to learn skills last year, for example?

In essence, we are proposing a two-pronged approach to helping people learn: create a positive climate for learning in the organisation, which is predominantly a responsibility of managers; and build up the learning capabilities of employees, groups and the organisation as a whole, which is a responsibility of both managers and HR. These two approaches are highly complementary. Whereas the climate for learning generates commitment, learning capabilities help to translate this into productive value for the organisation.

The shift from training to learning has many ramifications. It implies a need to re-evaluate the way we design interventions, leading to methods that consciously deepen the learning capabilities of employees, allowing them to take greater responsibility (individually and collectively) for their learning. Not all intervention methods currently achieve this, particularly those that rely too heavily on external expertise or content, rather than paying attention to the needs of the learner in their work context.

Although a proportion of conventional training courses could be interpreted as falling within this category, the shift to learning does not imply the end of training. As the Report demonstrates, training retains an important role in the learning organisation, if perhaps a more focused role than at present, and one that takes all possible steps in its design to cede responsibility for learning to employees.

The body of the Report is divided into the following four chapters:

◘ **Chapter 1 Why learning matters**

This chapter highlights some weaknesses of the conventional training model, in particular its tendency to emphasise subject-specific knowledge rather than seeking to build core learning abilities. It notes that distributed responsibility for learning is the only realistic way to ensure learning is relevant, timely and embedded within the work of employees. The chapter reviews the potential for learning to enhance the adaptive capacity of organisations – their ability to respond quickly and flexibly to changes in their operating environment. It also notes that not all learning is productive; and that success in building adaptive capacity depends on the strength of fit between an organisation's strategy and culture.

◘ **Chapter 2 The climate for learning**

This chapter introduces the concept of a growth medium – an organisational climate that generates commitment to a range of positive discretionary behaviours, including learning. The concept has its roots in a multitude of research studies on culture, climate and psychological well-being, stretching back more than thirty years. The chapter identifies three core conditions

underpinning the creation of a growth medium and proposes six leadership practices designed to help managers fulfil them.

◘ **Chapter 3 Learning how to learn**

This chapter explores the role of learning capabilities in preparing employees for the demands of the modern workplace. It highlights the need to move beyond the training paradigm towards approaches that enable employees to take responsibility for their own learning and embed learning practices more systematically within their work. The chapter offers a preliminary description of the capabilities needed to manage one's own learning; those needed to harness the learning potential of groups; and the skills needed to catalyse organisational change.

◘ **Chapter 4 Learning interventions**

This chapter explores the potential of interventions to help employees deepen their learning capabilities, allowing them to take greater responsibility (individually or collectively) for their own learning. It also notes the potential of some types of intervention to disrupt self-directed learning by paying insufficient attention to the needs of the learner in their work context. A number of specific roles for managers and HRD practitioners are proposed, designed to engage the learner in a discussion about their own situation and challenges.

1 | Why learning matters

- Learning enhances the adaptive capacity of an organisation – its ability to respond quickly and flexibly to changes in its operating environment.

- A poor fit between an organisation's strategy and culture causes the benefits of learning to be diffused.

- A powerful way to promote learning is to establish a positive psychological climate in which employees have the commitment to make their organisations more successful.

- By creating a positive climate for learning, supervisors, managers and HRD practitioners can deliver considerable strategic value to their organisation.

Introduction

Nobody need learn. Survival is not compulsory.
W. Edwards Deming, 1900–1993[1]

Few organisations could claim that their employees have the full range of capabilities necessary to deliver the company's vision. Fewer still could claim that they have sufficient capacity to respond to future changes in their operating environment. There always seems to be a gap.

The traditional response is to commission training courses. Yet, paradoxically, most people are aware of the limitations of this approach. Training has a tendency to react to present needs, rather than build capabilities for the future; to transfer large amounts of information, rather than build on the knowledge of participants; to remain detached from the context in which work is produced; and to lack the supporting processes needed to put new ideas into practice, with the result that the ideas are soon buried by more urgent priorities.

> I have had my concerns for some time about the impact we have as trainers. We turn up, do our bit (which is what the client asked for), realise that it is difficult to change things in a day (as this is mainly the way we all perform), then carry on, evaluate the outcome, talk to the client (if we can), and move on to the next job.
> *Roger Pattison, Consultant,*
> *Roger Pattison & Associates*

Attending a training course can feel similar to having a wheel changed on your car: a solution is provided and you are back on the road. But what if the road ahead is covered in oil or tacks, or runs over a cliff? Clearly you must fall back on your own experiences and judgements, and those of the people around you, but these core learning capabilities are not something that the course necessarily prepared you for.

> We can't train everyone to do everything. The emphasis is on getting people to learn within their work environment, and helping them to apply that knowledge.
> *Lorna McKee, Area HR Manager,*
> *Hilton Belfast*

In specialist domains there is also a further, more fundamental challenge to training interventions. The sheer amount of information and innovation being produced on a global scale means that the shelf-life of specialist knowledge is increasingly short. The time-lag between the delivery of a course and the need arising must be very short to avoid training materials becoming obsolete (Cunningham 2004). Chasing subject-specific

> '**The message for organisations is simple: cultivate learning everywhere, at all times, not only on training courses, and not only in response to perceived gaps in capability.**'

knowledge can become a full-time activity for the unwary training and development function.

Surely the answer is to design courses based on predicted future needs? Not so. The basic problems with the training model are not addressed by this approach. More significantly, there is no way of knowing what knowledge employees will require in five years' time. The only certainty is that conditions will be markedly different from today, and that new skill sets will be in demand.

Distributed ownership of learning, rather than dependency on centralised training provision, is the only realistic strategy for both parties in the training relationship, trainers and learners alike.[2] The message for organisations is simple: cultivate learning everywhere, at all times, not only on training courses, and not only in response to perceived gaps in capability.

The learning age

In the industrial age employees were hired to perform narrowly defined tasks in strictly controlled conditions. Management was viewed as a process of optimising output from employees and was undertaken by elite groups of managers and engineers. Learning time and variety were minimised, and repetitiveness was maximised. The organisation behaved like a large machine.

Nowadays the situation could not be more different. The twenty-first century knowledge worker is paid to apply technology, not be technology – and to orchestrate innovation, not maintain the status quo. There is a growing recognition that everyone – whatever level, function or location they inhabit – has a role to play in shaping the future of the organisation, a future of constant learning and change.

> Previously the investment has been in machinery; now the investment is in people.
> *Adrian Roberts, Personnel Manager, INA Bearing Company Ltd*

The factors producing change are many and widely reported: the relentless enlargement of markets, intensive global competition, rapid advances in technology, rising expectations of good conduct by society, and seemingly intractable environmental, social and security problems. The changing demographics of global population are also significant – an ageing and decreasing population in the wealthier nations, and a young and growing population elsewhere. The public sector contends with many of these issues while also seeking to adapt to a changing political landscape and chronic resource pressures.

Significant learning events in organisations often produce cultural changes and changes of outlook among employees. The visible benefits include fresh thinking, increased flexibility and responsiveness to external change. Organisations that foster a sense of commitment, pride and passion in their employees provide a solid platform for developing individual and organisational learning and, with it, performance. Organisations that understand the changing expectations of their stakeholders are more likely to survive in the long term. As Deming (1992) put it, 'The tide of innovation and change cannot be held back.'

Basic assumptions

Our previous study, *How do People Learn?*, examined the process of individual learning from four theoretical perspectives and attempted to demonstrate how they underpin modern training and development practice (CIPD 2002B). It also explored the differences between learning and training and, in particular, some of the limitations of instruction as a development method. The main observation of the report was that training and development practice has reached a critical stage in its evolution where the effectiveness of conventional methods such as instruction is being challenged, with new approaches appearing in their wake.

Three observations about learning shaped this view:

1   Learning is a more or less continuous process, occurring as we make sense of changes in our environment. It can happen at any time, anywhere, helping us to refine our actions in the light of unfolding sets of circumstances. Because learning arises out of our experience, it is personal, subjective and inseparable from activity. The idea that knowledge, the fruit of learning, can be 'imparted' from expert to novice (nowadays from computer to novice) is not supported by theoretical or empirical evidence. Receiving information does not equate to learning.[3] Although information can provide an important stimulus for learning, it must be acted upon in order to generate experience and learning. That process is largely self-directed.

2   Learning is socially mediated, ie strongly affected by the people around us. Experiments conducted throughout the twentieth century confirmed the fact that personal relationships, group[4] dynamics, cultural norms and the feeling (or lack of it) of social participation (belonging) all influence a person's appetite, and ability, to learn (for example, see Lewin

1947; Vygotsky 1962, 1978; Bandura 1977; Lave and Wenger 1991). A good deal of our experience – and hence learning – is driven by social activity, with few tasks accomplished in isolation from others. The simple act of observing more experienced colleagues can accelerate learning; conversing, swapping stories, co-operating on tasks and offering mutual support deepen and solidify the process. This kind of learning – often very informal in nature – is thought to be vastly more effective in building proficiency than more formalised training methods (Enos, Kehrrhahn and Bell 2003).

3   Learning is affected by a person's individual characteristics: their experience, relationships, aspirations, ability, level of confidence, particular situation and so on. These factors affect the speed, depth and creativity with which a person adapts to changes in their circumstances, sometimes of their own creation. If a person holds limiting assumptions about their potential or ability, this may cause them to aim low and overlook learning opportunities. Measures that increase the psychological well-being of employees (Schein 1999) are helpful in easing personal vulnerabilities, anxieties and blocks to learning.

> The human condition is such that we suffer from things like self-doubt and we remain affected by our past experiences long after the event.
> *Graham O'Connell, CMPS, Cabinet Office*

These observations suggest that learning is a lifelong process that transcends any particular time or circumstances, and that learning can take place

> **'Learning leads to adaptations in the behaviour of employees that, if properly aligned...will enable the organisation to deliver greater value to its stakeholders.'**

in any situation where experience is gathered, from reading a book to holding a conversation, and from climbing a mountain to working on a business problem, or practically any other human endeavour. As David Kolb wrote in his 1984 study (p. 32):

Learning is the major process of human adaptation.

The observations also highlight two possible constraints on learning: our own anxieties about growth and development; and the support for learning (or lack of it) that we receive from the people and environment around us.

Adaptive capacity

The modern organisation is buffeted by interest groups – customers, investors, regulators, employees, competitors, communities and campaigners – and must learn how to sustain their trust through difficult and complex times. The capability to understand these forces, pre-empt problems and seize opportunities ahead of the competition is indispensable to organisations. It allows them to *sustain (and enhance) the flow of value to their stakeholders*.

The case for learning could not be more solid. *Learning leads to adaptations in the behaviour of employees that, if properly aligned with group and corporate goals, will enable the organisation to deliver greater value to its stakeholders*. The problem is that such alignment cannot be taken for granted and certainly cannot be created by executive decree. Where alignment is weak, efforts to promote learning may deliver significant benefit to individual learners but may not contribute strategically to the organisation.

For alignment to occur, the environment in which learning takes place (the 'climate' for learning) must provide employees with the right mix of inspiration, incentive and support to channel their learning in a direction that is beneficial to the organisation. At the heart of this challenge lies the often-overlooked issue of organisational culture, and its role in determining employee attitudes to learning and change.

Ideally, decisions agreed by senior managers would be put into practice quickly by managers at other levels, leading to measurable improvements in organisational performance. The organisation would be perfectly agile – the strategic imperatives of the organisation (as envisioned by its senior managers) would be accepted by others immediately without inertia or resistance, allowing the success of the decisions to be measured by hard performance data – the chief executive's dream.

In reality, the influence of culture is always present – the history, values, norms and beliefs of the organisation, entwined with its systems and policies. As Figure 1, opposite, illustrates, decisions made at the top (or centre) may be greeted with suspicion, cynicism and indifference at other levels, such that impacts vary according to the degree of personal buy-in to the decisions. Bureaucratic systems, perverse reward systems and a lack of understanding of the issues (all integral parts of the organisation's culture) dissipate the impacts further, making it almost impossible to attribute performance changes to strategy – the chief executive's nightmare.

Two extreme scenarios, admittedly, but they make the point that change initiatives are underpinned by processes of learning and that the quality of

'Adaptive capacity is the greatest gift of learning. It allows an organisation to remain agile in the face of uncertain future conditions...'

Figure 1 | The impact of culture on organisational strategy

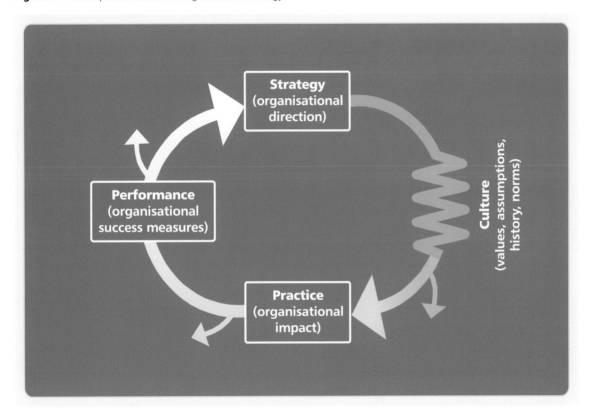

those processes is dependent on the degree to which the strategy resonates with the culture of the organisation. Cultures that evolve in tandem with the strategic needs of an organisation demonstrate *adaptive capacity*; those that do not can become rigid and unresponsive. The main factor differentiating the two is the ability of employees (and the groups in which they work) to align their learning with the strategic needs of the organisation.

Adaptive capacity is the greatest gift of learning. It allows an organisation to remain agile in the face of uncertain future conditions, whereas other outcomes of learning, such as new knowledge and

skills, tend to have specific applications and a shorter shelf-life. Not surprisingly, Kotter and Heskett (1992, p. 53) have been able to show that organisations with a strong 'adaptive core' produce more robust economic performance:

When something in the firm's context changes – such as the level of competition – managers are quick to spot this trend... If changes in the firm's strategies and practices are needed in order to respond to new contextual conditions, even practices rooted in the culture, those initiatives continue until the cultural changes are made. In this way, managers help maintain a fit between the culture and its context.

What drives learning?

Because learning is an instrumental activity, it depends above all on people making decisions to act to improve their situation, including their performance at work. The decision to act, to seek a goal, to create something new, sets the learning process in motion. Without human agency in the process, learning would remain unfocused, without direction. To this extent, improvement and learning are causally related: obtain the will to improve, and the process of learning will follow.[5]

So how does the will to improve arise? Under authoritarian or close-supervision regimes, management obtains it through the exercise of power and control. The aim is to modify employee behaviours until they suit the needs of the organisation. In contrast, under people-centred regimes, attempts are made to liberate agency rather than have it enforced. There is a recognition that humans are inherently productive under the right conditions.

> People should participate in the learning process as enthusiastic volunteers rather than because they are told to do so.
> *Russell Devitt, Partner, Acuition*

These two perspectives on human behaviour – referred to as Theory X and Theory Y – were popularised by Douglas McGregor in the 1950s. McGregor's work is important from a learning perspective, since the two theories result in quite different forms of learning strategy. Theory X leads to a strategy of top-down goal-setting, close supervision and behavioural modification through training, such that the learner develops a direction decided by the organisation. The drawback of this

approach is that responsibility for learning remains beyond the control of the employee and is therefore dependent on external intervention, which can be costly, late and ineffective. It is also inefficient to manage learning separately from work, since this creates the need for a 'transfer' process.

Learning strategies based upon Theory Y focus on the psychological climate of the organisation (the personal sense of well-being arising through participation in work), which has been shown to influence employee attitudes to organisational improvement (Payne 2002). Instead of teaching employees the things that the organisation believes they should know, this approach encourages them to direct their own affairs within a supportive learning environment. That environment may consist of management practices that place a high value on learning, and group processes that create and sustain commitment to organisational improvement. In McGregor's words (McGregor 1966, p. 15),

the essential task of management is to arrange organizational conditions and methods of operation so that people can achieve their own goals best by directing their own efforts toward organizational objectives.

Summary

This chapter highlighted some weaknesses of the conventional training model, in particular its tendency to emphasise subject-specific knowledge, rather than seeking to build core learning abilities. It noted that distributed responsibility for learning is the only realistic way to ensure learning is relevant, timely and embedded within the work of employees.

The discussion reviewed the potential for learning to enhance the adaptive capacity of organisations

'**By creating a positive *climate for learning*, supervisors, managers and HRD practitioners can deliver considerable strategic value to their organisation.'**

– their ability to respond quickly and flexibly to changes in their operating environment. It was noted that not all learning is productive. In particular, success in building adaptive capacity was recognised to depend on the degree of fit between an organisation's strategy and culture, a weak fit causing the benefits of learning to be diffused.

The discussion went on to explore the driving forces behind learning, concluding that in instances where the learning is of benefit to an organisation, they are similar in character to the forces driving organisational improvement. This led to the conclusion that a powerful way to promote learning in organisations is to establish a positive psychological climate in which employees are drawn to learning through a commitment to make their organisations more successful.

By creating a positive *climate for learning*, supervisors, managers and HRD practitioners can deliver considerable strategic value to their organisation. Yet the approach is comparatively

underdeveloped as a learning strategy in organisations. This subject forms the focus of Chapter 2.

Endnotes

1   Deming (1992).

2   Too much dependency on external expertise can be damaging for learning. One of the most startling comments we came across during our previous study was from a manager in a telecommunications company who had asked an employee what they had learned that day: 'Nothing,' replied the employee, 'I haven't been on a training course since last year.'

3   The receipt of information does not always lead to awareness, and greater awareness does not always lead to changes in behaviour. A complex web of factors determines whether or not a person 'hears' a message, finds it relevant, and acts upon it. This lesson is most amply demonstrated in the failure of certain mass communications programmes (see Collins *et al* 2003).

4   The word group is intended to range from individual relationships through to teams, committees, clubs, networks, alliances, communities of practice and, in principle, whole organisations.

5   That is, learning of value to the organisation as opposed to learning of sole value to the employee.

Questions for your organisation

◘   Is your organisation preparing itself for the future? How can you ensure that it adapts and grows as its operating conditions change?

◘   How easily do people respond to change – with eagerness or trepidation? How can you help to make the culture more adaptive?

◘   How well do senior managers understand the link between learning and strategy implementation? Behind the rhetoric, is learning perceived to be a strategic issue?

◘   How can you ensure that individual and team learning is aligned with your organisation's objectives? What processes can you use?

2 | Creating a climate for learning

You can make people go to workshops, but you can't get them to learn something they don't want to learn. What will draw people into a learning process? Our experience is that the desire to learn and improve is intrinsically driven and realised through conditions which an organization creates for its employees.

George Roth and Art Kleiner[1]

◘ Learning can be cultivated by management practices that raise commitment among employees, creating what might be described as an organisational 'growth medium'.

◘ The logic of the growth medium is simple: in the right climate, employees will commit to a range of positive discretionary behaviours, including learning.

◘ Since the climate for learning is determined largely by managers, the latter play a pivotal role in facilitating the learning of their staff.

◘ Three core challenges lie behind the development of a growth medium: give employees a sense of purpose in the workplace; grant employees opportunities to act upon their commitment; and offer practical support for learning.

◘ While a positive climate for learning is important, it is not sufficient to deliver the full benefits of learning to an organisation. The missing ingredient is learning capabilities.

Introduction

Recent research commissioned by the CIPD confirms what many HRD practitioners have always suspected: practices that build employee commitment lead to positive 'discretionary

behaviours' that are necessary for job and organisational success (CIPD 2003D). According to Sloman (2003), one of the most important forms of discretionary behaviour is *discretionary learning*, where individuals actively seek to acquire the knowledge and skills that promote the organisation's objectives.

> Discretionary behaviour is the key. This is where management and managers must work not just to deliver results but to create an environment where individuals and teams can and will commit.
> *Rob Field, Training and Development Manager, Avis Europe plc*

The CIPD study links discretionary behaviour to employee ability, degree of motivation and level of opportunity to make their contribution to the organisation felt, and is hence termed the 'AMO' model. The work correlates well with other studies of employee commitment in the work psychology literature which, more broadly, have sought to model the factors giving rise to employee psychological well-being.[2]

Commitment can be understood as the set of *motivating* forces that drive an employee to add value to their organisation through their participation in work, teams, networks and other work-based structures. Committed employees will seek to excel at what they do – that is the direction in which they apply their discretionary behaviour. They will wish to remain affiliated with their organisation, accept its values and goals, and push the boundaries of their experience as they exert effort on its behalf (Schultz and Schultz 1998, p. 268; CIPD 2002A). Commitment unleashes the energy to tackle organisational tasks, while

> '**Commitment unleashes the energy to tackle organisational tasks, while learning ensures that they can be carried out effectively.**'

learning ensures that they can be carried out effectively.

The psychology of motivation has attracted a vast body of literature over the years, much of which was reviewed in CIPD (2002B, p. 34). Although motivation has been modelled in many different ways, there is a broad consensus that the factors illustrated in Table 1 exert a significant pull on employees in the work setting.[3] While each person will rank the factors differently, practices that enable employees to meet these intrinsic needs can be expected to enhance commitment. As Robert Kaplan and David Norton (1996, p. 136) note:

Table 1 | Sources of workplace motivation

Achievement: the sense that work will lead to fulfilment through the accomplishment of work goals.	**Growth and development**: the sense that new capabilities will result from participation in work activities.
Advancement: the sense that good performance will be rewarded by added responsibility, status or promotion in the organisation.	**Intellectual interest**: the sense that work activities will coincide with personal areas of interest.
Belonging: the feeling of fulfilment, pride and loyalty obtained by working with other people on common challenges.	**Job security**: the sense that good performance will lead to a more longer-lasting work opportunity.
Challenge: the sense that work activities will be exciting and stimulating.	**Pride in organisation**: the sense of pleasure taken in associating with the organisation, based on its reputation, culture and policies.
Contribution to society: the feeling that work makes a worthwhile contribution to society, adding meaning and purpose to everyday actions.	**Recognition and respect**: the sense that contributions will be acknowledged and appreciated by colleagues.
Involvement: the sense of ownership over work objectives arising from the freedom to act under one's own initiative and to participate in decisions.	**Responsibility**: the care and commitment flowing from the management of people and involvement in decisions.
Financial reward: the sense that good performance will be rewarded by greater financial benefits.	**Work environment**: the sense of well-being produced by the physical surroundings of the workplace.

Even skilled employees, provided with superb information, will not contribute to organizational success if they are not motivated to act in the best interests of the organization or if they are not given freedom to make decisions and take actions.

Inevitably, every workplace also contains factors that can breed dissatisfaction, sap interest in work and diminish commitment. These are Herzberg's so-called 'hygiene' factors (Herzberg, Mausner and Snyderman 1959). Many can be identified by flipping the positive factors around: absence of opportunities for advancement, growth or recognition, exclusion from decisions, ineptness of organisation, unfair policies, poor pay and conditions, and so on. Herzberg discovered that they had a more durable (and negative) impact on motivation than the positive factors. Attempts to boost commitment to learning and performance in the workplace must begin with their removal.

The growth medium

The idea that learning can be cultivated by organisational practices that raise commitment among employees has profound consequences for people development. It suggests that a climate of supervision and training – however professionally implemented – may fail to engage employees at a fundamental level. Coaxing performance out of uncommitted employees will at best achieve short-lived results and, in the case of failed change initiatives, can rebound. As Roth and Kleiner (2000, p. 205) observe,

The learner learns what the learner wants to learn.

If Senge likens the top-down approach in people development to a mechanic fixing a car, he likens the new organic model to gardening (Senge 1999). He points out that you cannot stand over plants imploring them, 'Grow! Try harder! You can do it!' If a plant is not provided with the right physical ingredients, 'There's nothing anyone can do to make a difference.' That is not to say that there is a standard solution to gardening – in fact diversity is one of its most attractive features. But whatever practices are adopted the basic conditions for growth must be present. To borrow a phrase from biology, an organisation should take a close look at its 'growth medium' before assuming that its problems are due to an intrinsic lack of competency or motivation among its employees.

The logic of the growth medium is simple: in the right climate, employees will be motivated to pursue a range of positive discretionary behaviours, including learning. Since the climate for learning is determined largely by managers, this model suggests that managers can play a pivotal role in facilitating the learning of their staff.

Following a review of the literature,[4] three conditions have been identified that organisations need to meet in order to build a growth medium (see Figure 2 on page 12):

1 *Employees must go into work with a sense of purpose*. It is not sufficient to assume that this is provided by narrowly defined organisational objectives such as profitability, stock price and market share, despite their universality. A strong sense of purpose can help to maintain focus in uncertain or volatile operating conditions. It can bring coherence to otherwise isolated or conflicting decisions and help to forge a sense of shared identity among employees.

2 *Employees must be provided with opportunities to turn their commitment into productive*

'**Because so much learning occurs directly through work, managers should aim to include these responsibilities within their normal repertoire of behaviours...**'

Figure 2 | The three conditions of the growth medium

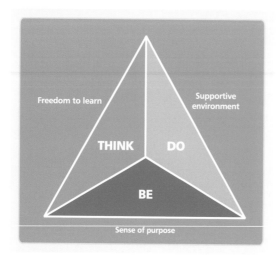

action. That means giving them the freedom to organise their work and learning affairs, with role models to follow, rather than imposing a culture of supervision and training. This is largely a question of management style – the degree to which the talents of employees are either liberated or boxed in.

3   *Employees must sense that they are working within a supportive learning environment.* Encouragement from managers and peers is crucial, as is the presence of policies and systems that encourage learning behaviours. Even the most purposeful, self-directed learner, whose instinct is to explore, experiment and engage with work activities to create value for their organisation, will benefit from time and support for their learning.

To the extent that the elements of the 'growth medium' have been studied, theorised and tested in organisations throughout the last 60 years, this is by no means a radical approach. But to many organisations – even ones that have sought to

develop a growth medium for many years – the task still represents a significant developmental challenge.

Management practices

Table 2 (opposite) highlights a variety of responsibilities for managers that flow out of the three growth-medium conditions. The objective is to help managers create the conditions in which learning and improvement can prosper, by appealing to the sources of motivation held most highly by employees.

The table also highlights a reciprocal set of responsibilities for employees, designed to take advantage of the evolving climate for learning established by managers. The interdependent nature of these responsibilities suggests that the growth medium is viewed as a 'learning partnership' between managers and employees.

Because so much learning occurs directly through work, managers should aim to include these responsibilities within their normal repertoire of behaviours, rather than view them as separate learning activities. *For that reason, they may be viewed as leadership practices that promote learning, rather than learning practices that enhance specific knowledge and skills, and hence justify mainstream attention.*

Based upon the responsibilities in Table 2, the remainder of this section outlines six practices for managers that are designed to establish a growth medium.

Practice 1: Develop the vision

Without a mental picture of the probable conditions in which we shall find ourselves in

Table 2 | Responsibilities of managers and employees

	Managers	Employees
Sense of purpose *Develop and share a vision*	Keep abreast of the changing conditions in which your organisation operates. Contribute to the development of the organisation's vision and strategy. Bring the vision to life by expressing it in ways that are clear to employees.	Be aware of the organisation's vision and strategic needs. Confirm your understanding of its vision and strategy with others. Participate fully in group decisions. Fulfil commitments to your group.
Freedom to learn *Empower employees and lead by example*	Enable and encourage, rather than control. Develop coaching capacity. Encourage reflection. Unlock enquiry skills rather than teach staff how to behave. Maintain and demonstrate personal commitment to learning.	Take control of your learning and development. Look on work challenges as learning opportunities, and practise critical reflection on work outcomes. Contribute to team development as much as your own.
Supportive environment *Encourage networks and align organisational systems*	Encourage employees to share their knowledge. Champion the use of peer-to-peer networks. Ensure such networks are effective through 'light touch' facilitation. Ensure that the organisation's policies and systems remain in alignment with its vision.	Identify the networks in which you operate. Support them by contributing ideas and knowledge for others. Offer support for improvements in the design of policies and systems.

future, planning can descend into a daily fight for survival. This is why sense-making – the art of helping people to detect and understand 'emerging futures' – is so important to the learning process and, by implication, to organisations.

> Last year we launched our brand promise and values. The aim was to establish a clear set of values around customer service in keeping with our brand image, which all employees would understand. This was to help us direct all our actions to the same end, and develop a way of being with each other and our customers that we want everyone to recognise, appreciate and want more of.
>
> *Melissa Cockrill, Training Officer,*
> *Harvey Nichols, Edinburgh*

The problem is that our ability to anticipate and plan for future circumstances is usually constrained by the shortage of time and resources, or by the apparent inertia of the organisation around us. Helping people to inject a longer time-horizon into their decision-making, rather than applying quick fixes to hazily understood circumstances, is therefore as much a leadership skill as a learning skill.

The collective sense-making of an organisation is often described as its vision or 'big idea', which Mike Pedler and his colleagues (Pedler, Burgoyne and Boydell 1991, p. 109) define as the 'hope for and belief in a desired future' – in other words, a picture of 'what success looks like' for every employee, that grips the imagination and invokes a passion for action. The CIPD's recent study on people and performance confirms the positive effect of a 'big idea' on employee attitudes towards their organisation (CIPD 2003D).

Shared vision among teams, communities, organisations, political parties, etc is thought to breed shared commitment, resulting in synergistic actions and effort on the part of group members. The capacity to unite people around shared goals makes vision an important factor in furthering organisational development. As change specialist John Kotter notes (1996, p. 85):

A great vision can serve a useful purpose even if it is understood by just a few people. But the real power of a vision is unleashed only when most of those involved in an enterprise activity have a common understanding of its goals and direction. That shared sense of a desirable future can help motivate and coordinate the kinds of actions that create transformations.

A good vision is believed in by employees. It may be co-created by employees through a participative process, or built intuitively upon their beliefs, values and norms – in short, upon their identity. Above all, a good vision paints a positive, achievable picture for employees, that builds on the qualities they most value in the organisation. Visions that do not engage employees at an emotional level can produce apathy, resentment and alienation among them – even when they were prepared for otherwise sound business reasons.

As Kotter (1992) reminds us, however, the object of a vision is not purely to breed cohesiveness among staff: it must also be *strategically correct* for the organisation. No amount of enthusiasm will protect an organisation from a flawed vision. Thus, as well as employees, the vision must pay attention to the needs of other stakeholders, such as customers, shareholders, regulators and voices within civil society. The challenge for vision builders is to remain alive to the organisation's strategic context while building on its core culture and identity.

Practice 2: Share the vision

No vision will be equally attractive to all employees, and organisations are better off for the diversity this implies. At the personal scale, an organisation whose vision is 'to become the market leader in low-emission vehicle engines' might inspire those interested in design excellence and global warming. Big ideas around shareholder return, bonuses or economic growth might capture the attention of people whose interests are predominantly financial. The values embodied by a vision are bound to attract different degrees of emotional 'buy-in' from employees.

> As we embarked on building a dynamic, successful business, it was essential that we had everyone pulling together towards the same shared goals.
> *Clive Wilson, Managing Director, Primeast*

Nonetheless, the vision must carry the majority of employees along in its wake if it is to cause the organisation to 'tip' in the desired direction. By exploring how the vision intersects with their staff's existing goals, and how the two may be brought into better alignment, managers play a critical role in this process.

Alignment at group level is also essential. As far back as the 1940s, Kurt Lewin discovered that it was extremely hard to change a person's pattern of behaviour independently of the groups in which they operate: the person reverts back quickly to the group 'norm'. By implication, decisions made in a group setting can produce a more powerful and

sustained commitment to action than individual decisions, or ones imposed on the group from 'outside' (see Lewin 1947; Marrow 1969; Likert 1984). Lewin summarised this phenomenon as follows (Marrow 1969, p. 144):

Motivation alone does not suffice to lead to change. This link is provided by decisions. A process like decision-making, which only takes a few minutes, is able to affect conduct for many months to come.

Every manager will take a different approach to sharing the organisation's vision with their team. As well as the manager's individual leadership style, the group's interest in making the vision their own may depend on any or all of the following factors:

◘ The conviction (and consistency) with which the vision is seen to be held by senior management.

◘ How 'local' the vision is to the group, in terms of its members' involvement in establishing the big idea, goals, values etc. When the vision is not local, how amenable is it to local interpretation?

◘ How easily the vision can be grasped and translated into practical actions by group members.

◘ Whether they feel able to fulfil their individual contribution, based upon the current capabilities and resources of the group.

◘ How well the group is perceived to function as a team, in terms of its shared values, sense of loyalty, aspiration and openness to new ideas.

As Senge (1999, p. 178) points out, the real value of a vision is its capacity to provide an umbrella under which people can participate in interesting and rewarding work of strategic value to the organisation:

People don't necessarily want to 'have a vision' at work… They want to be part of a team that's fun to work with and that produces results they are proud of.

For many, then, the *way* that a vision is brought to life in an organisation is more important than the details of the vision itself, for this reflects the true values of the organisation. When the espoused intentions of the organisation are not borne out in practice, a serious brake is placed on commitment. How many people could remain passionate about a company that tolerates sexist or racist practices, mistreats its suppliers, dumps waste on its local communities or defrauds its investors while trumpeting its contribution to society?

O'Reilly and Pfeffer's (2000) research suggests that employees whose personal values are aligned with those of their organisation demonstrate a higher degree of motivation, stay longer and will work more productively than other employees. The implication is that commitment is not only driven by intellectual, goal-based visions of the future but also by emotional, values-based concerns about the journey there.

> Managers need to develop their staff and not view this as a 'bolt-on' activity, exclusively for HR.
> *Steve Butcher, Learning and Development Adviser, Petroleum Development Oman*

Practice 3: Empower employees

The freedom to organise work, make decisions and initiate learning can be profoundly motivating for employees. At root this requires managers to trust employees to act upon their own initiative, albeit within certain boundaries (the 'non-negotiables' or 'hard rules' governing employee conduct), and with the offer of support always on hand. Argyris (1990, pp. 33–4) views the commitment so gained in terms of an increase in an employee's 'psychological success' – something he believes may be encouraged by providing:

opportunities for work in which the individual is able to define his immediate goals, define his own paths to these goals, relate these to the goals of the organization, evaluate his own effectiveness, and constantly increase the degree of challenge at work.

There is growing evidence to suggest that many 'ordinary' employees, with no particular fast-track or 'high-potential' status, can perform well above their normal level once they take ownership of a vision and are allowed to manage their work and learning activities (O'Reilly and Pfeffer 2000). Decisions that would otherwise have been left to managers are made locally, and independently, freeing employees (and, at the next rung, teams) to use their initiative, and freeing managers to think strategically. A climate of 'supported autonomy' can be particularly effective when combined with high expectations of performance from managers.[5]

It must be said that not all employees are ready for empowerment, and not all of them would wish to accept it even if they were. This is a separate issue that may be addressed through coaching or may require a deeper process of development planning. Suffice to say that empowerment is not a universal

> **'Learning is best promoted through a facilitative style of management in which responsibility for decision-making is ceded as far as possible to the employee.'**

motivator for all employees. Most would agree, however, that there are few situations more demotivating than a breakdown of trust with a manager, which may result in the latter 'taking over' an employee's work, marginalising their contribution and setting low standards on attainment.

Learning is best promoted through a facilitative style of management in which responsibility for decision-making is ceded as far as possible to the employee. In practice, this must occur within a supportive atmosphere where learning capabilities can be discovered and applied, and where displays of learning are recognised and rewarded (financially or otherwise). The management style associated most closely with facilitation is *coaching*. In contrast to more directive approaches, coaching aims to grow capabilities as well as 'get the job done'. Caplan (2003, p. 20) describes the coaching style of management in the following way:

One where the managers use coaching techniques in their discussions and dealings with staff. Through these techniques a manager encourages the employees to identify options and seek their own solutions to problems. This style is in direct contrast to a directive one where the manager has the answer and tells the employee how it should be done…

The comparative withdrawal of supervision must be balanced by the provision of time, resources, information and, crucially, feedback in order to guide employees through their work challenges. Without this they may feel at sea and disregarded. Coaching does not imply a 'laissez-faire' approach to management. The aim is to establish an environment in which employees are trusted to learn and succeed, not simply to devolve responsibilities.

> The message that training is by no means the only or best way to promote learning is very important. A coaching approach to learning and development tries to emphasise that managers should look much more broadly for how to meet learning needs.
> *Andy Cooke, Coaching and Mentoring Consultant for Shell EP*

The goal of the coach is to draw out the talents of others. A typical exchange creates clarity and moves the employee closer to action. It accelerates the employee's progress by providing greater focus and awareness of choice. As they coach, managers should learn to recognise and appreciate progress as it occurs, and take steps to overcome bottlenecks to learning, such as fuzziness of vision, group dysfunction or constraints embedded in the organisation's structures or systems (for a more detailed discussion see CIPD 2004A).

Progress towards a 'coaching culture' will depend on subtle changes in outlook among managers and cannot just be switched on. As Caley and Reid (2003, p. 37) point out, there is a need for clarity about coaching practices, and decent support processes for managers themselves:

Many managers are willing to undertake a role in supporting learning, but are unclear of what is expected of them. It has to be recognised that supervisors themselves frequently lack support to enable them to perform adequately in the role of coach and mentor, and their performance is not infrequently judged against different criteria. This may run counter to their inclination and the needs of those they supervise.

Practice 4: Lead by example

Humans are adept at learning from each other. This instinctive capability is demonstrated by children almost the moment they are born as they begin to imitate the sounds and smiles of their parents. The process continues long into adulthood as new situations call for new behaviours that may be observed among colleagues in the first instance. 'Observational learning', as Bandura (1977) called it, not only saves time but also reduces the risk of embarrassing or dangerous mistakes.

It is not surprising therefore that innovative people have a disproportionately large impact on their organisations. They are the ones to watch, the ones that unfreeze old behaviours, define new norms and set new standards by example. Schein (1999, p. 125) considers that, in acting as beacons for others to follow, positive role models are an essential condition for learning and change:

The new way of thinking and behaving may be so different that you must see what it looks like before you can imagine yourself doing it. You must be able to see the new behavior and attitudes in others with whom you can identify.

> If employees think there is no trust or support in the working and learning environment, then the organisation's vision and values become less meaningful.
> *David Jones, Manager Group Learning Services, HSBC Learning and Development*

A good role model will project a sense of confidence, even delight, in the way they seek change, allowing others to follow in their wake.

But while the sense of excitement this brings is extremely valuable, it may not be sufficient to solidify new patterns of behaviour. A true role model will go one step further, demonstrating how new ideas can be made to work in practice, and how the factors working to maintain the status quo can be overcome.

On a daily basis, managers have the greatest potential to provide a role model for their team. It is not surprising, then, that recent research from the CIPD confirms the pivotal role of managers in delivering (some would say 'living') the requirements of the organisation (CIPD 2003D, p. 8; see also CIPD 2003B):

Organisational culture and values are often experienced by workers through the behaviour of front-line managers in the way these managers show respect, exhibit trust, respond to suggestions, give directions, and behave. We call this front-line leadership since in effect front-line managers have a crucial role in translating policies and practices, and wider cultures and values, into actions.

> We are learning from employees by encouraging them to participate in an ideas bank that is linked to our six areas of strategic focus. Employees contribute ideas, tell us which area of the business they believe it will improve, and how it may work, and we reward ideas used and share them across the group.
> *Rob Field, Training and Development Manager, Avis Europe plc*

As an example, imagine working for an organisation that suffers from a culture of micro-management, suppression of initiative and tight

> **'...peer connection offers a way to support learning that is superior to conventional top-down solutions.'**

control of information. A role model would approach this challenge by attempting to outperform other managers through the use of a coaching style of management, gaining the respect of their team at the same time. If successful, the example could have much greater influence on the organisation than negative stories about failure, inefficiency and blame. Clearly, leading by example may require the manager to work across the grain of the organisation's culture periodically, but in a positive way that fully supports the organisation's long-term interests.

Characteristics of an innovative manager include a questioning approach to work challenges; a willingness to query old assumptions before supporting quick fixes; an openness to ideas from all sources; and encouragement of critical reflection on work outcomes. In this way they create a climate of enquiry among their team, where success and failure are characterised by their learning potential: errors are regarded as learning opportunities, and successes as measures of personal development. Fear of failure is actively discouraged owing to its inhibiting effect on learning.

Practice 5: Encourage networks

Ideas and the inspiration for action can emerge anywhere in an organisation, not just from the top strata or specialists at the centre. Some of the best thinking can arise among employees in outward-facing roles who detect changes in customer requirements, or who are exposed to learning opportunities among suppliers and partners. These people may not have the expertise or resources to bring alive their ideas directly; nor may they know about similar ideas emerging in other quarters of the organisation.

One of the tasks of a manager is to facilitate the flow of information across organisational boundaries such that ideas, expertise and resources are pooled rather than duplicated or ignored. Vertically organised management systems are not always efficient at doing this. They tend to breed gatekeepers who, even unintentionally, slow down or even block the flow of information. It is thus fashionable for organisations to complement or even replace hierarchical structures with informal management structures based around more *lateral* connections. Self-managed teams, peer networks and communities of practice are examples.

> Important sources of knowledge are locked up in the organisation's relationships with its stakeholders (eg its customers and suppliers).
> *Russell Devitt, Partner, Acuition*

The best cases of peer support are driven by business need. Brown and Duguid's (1991) analysis of Orr's (1990) study of Xerox service technicians reveals that a community of practice was born out of a mutual need to share problem-solving experiences. BP's 'peer assist' and 'peer challenge' processes give managers the opportunity to gain essential insights into the merit of their future plans. In both cases peer connection offers a way to support learning that is superior to conventional top-down solutions.

Community is a subtle concept. Simply labelling people as members of this group or that network, even when supported by websites, contact directories and registers of expertise, does not create community. Attempts to create it in the organisation's image can easily backfire, as communities exist to serve the interests of their members, not the organisation's goals. As Brown and Duguid (1991) note:

communities-of-practice must be allowed some latitude to shake themselves free of received wisdom.

> Networking, both formal and informal, can help people see problems from different angles, and come up with innovative solutions. Mentors can also help point the way. Networks outside the organisation may bring benefits and more fresh approaches. It is a form of knowledge management that does not rely on databases.
> *David Laughrin, Director, dblearning*

As well as their role in supporting informal learning, peer networks can breed a sense of shared identity across organisational boundaries, helping to glue the organisation together by weeding out duplicated effort, sharing knowledge and harmonising disparate approaches.

Further coherence can be achieved through other types of lateral connection and community. The existence of standardised services like computer networks, communication systems and information resources affirms corporate identity while avoiding the need (and cost) of managing multiple services at the local level. However, as Ghoshal and Gratton (2002, p. 36) point out, operational integration is not a substitute for the stronger, deeper forms of integration facilitated by peer connections:

Fluid and flexible collective action requires not only standardized infrastructure, shared knowledge and mutual trust, but also emotional integration through a common purpose and identity.

Driven by the needs of their members, peer networks are largely self-organising. Managers can help to sustain them in several important ways, however. They can lend credibility to the networks by participating in them fully and acting upon suggestions. They can celebrate group successes, champion their value among senior managers and ensure that they receive the resources necessary to be effective.

Practice 6: Align policies and systems

The policies and systems of an organisation give physical expressions to its underlying culture. If the culture is static, the policies and systems will be static. If the culture is adaptive, the systems will be assessed regularly to ensure they deliver value to the organisation. Systems that throw up problems rather than facilitate work can have a serious dampening effect on learning, in extreme cases leading to a sense of powerlessness. Caley and Reid (2003, p. 41) describe the potential effects on employees:

Bureaucracy within any organisation leads to a feeling of frustration on the part of many workers, who feel that they have limited influence on the change agenda. In environments where there is also pressure to meet targets, and work is primarily task-focused, this can lead to a negative culture that breeds a just-in-time mentality.

Examples of dysfunction include overbearing management systems that enslave people in bureaucracy, or time-management systems that inhibit discussion by demanding that every minute of every day is assigned to a cost centre. Such systems may have been established with worthy intentions – customer service quality and resource monitoring respectively – but have grown apart from organisational needs.

While bureaucratic systems can dampen learning, systems that work against the organisation's professed direction are more damaging. There is often a gap between the values of the organisation as espoused by its senior managers and the real ways in which decisions are made. Every culture throws up its anomalies, but organisations that embed them in policies and systems reveal their inconsistency most clearly to employees.

Take the example of the manager who leaves their staff in no doubt that long working hours are essential for career advancement, while the organisation's values stress the importance of work–life balance. Or the competency framework that makes no reference to environmental management, while the company communicates its green commitments. Schein (1999, pp. 125–6) offers a framework for developing teamworking:

If you are learning how to be a team player, the reward system must be group-oriented, the discipline system must punish individually aggressive and selfish behavior, and the organizational structures must make it possible to work as a team.

Kotter (1996) highlights HR systems – notably performance evaluation, compensation, promotion, recruitment and training systems – as being particularly sensitive to misalignment. If such systems are allowed to become remote from, or conflict with, organisational strategy, then a sense

of unease or cynicism with the systems can follow. As Kotter (1996, p. 111) notes, the impression that managers are content with the systems can be strongly disempowering for employees:

When the big, built-in, hard-wired incentives and processes are seriously at odds with the new vision, you must deal with that fact directly. Dodging the issue disempowers employees and risks undermining the change.

By contrast, if managers are perceived to be aware of the limitations of existing systems, and are seen to be actively engaged in their renewal, the effect on staff can be positive and empowering.

Summary

This chapter introduced the concept of a growth medium – an organisational climate that generates commitment to a range of positive discretionary behaviours, including learning. The concept has its roots in a multitude of research studies on culture, climate and psychological well-being stretching back more than thirty years.

Three core challenges lie behind the development of a growth medium. Because the challenges are mutually dependent, they are more accurately described as 'conditions' for establishing a successful climate for learning:

1 *Create a sense of purpose in the workplace.* Not all learning is valuable to organisations. The fundamental challenge of the growth medium is to create employee commitment around the organisation's core vision and values, such that their sense of purpose drives the interests of the organisation. From this, many other things fall into alignment, including learning.

> '**Practical support for learning in the form of peer networks, supportive policies and systems, and protected time for learning, is necessary even for the most committed and self-directed employee.'**

2 *Give employees the opportunity to act upon their commitment*. In order to create productive value for the organisation, employees must be given the freedom to organise their work and learning activities, all within a framework of clear boundaries and rules established by the organisation.

3 *Provide employees with a supportive learning environment*. Practical support for learning in the form of peer networks, supportive policies and systems, and protected time for learning, is necessary even for the most committed and self-directed employee.

Using the three conditions as a starting point, the discussion then introduced six management practices which, taken together, are designed to create these conditions. The background to each practice was explored, offering managers a clearer assessment of the requirements for building a growth medium.

Notwithstanding the power of a growth medium to motivate learning, seasoned HRD practitioners will know that it is not sufficient by itself to deliver the full benefits of learning to the organisation. The missing ingredient is *learning capabilities*, the subject of the next chapter.

Endnotes

1 Roth and Kleiner (2000, p. 205).

2 See Warr (2002) for a good summary.

3 Factors such as hunger, thirst, shelter, safety and love are not included, as the model assumes that these are being met outside the organisation. In oppressive or unstable societies this may not always be the case.

4 An early analysis of 'organisational climate' was offered by Litwin and Stringer (1968). This has remained an active field of research (see Ashkanasy *et al* 2000 for a good summary), with many nuances and branches. Work by Schein (1999) and Senge *et al* (1999) capture many of its themes in studies of organisational culture and learning respectively.

5 For a review of the so-called 'Pygmalion Effect' see Livingston (2003).

Questions for your organisation

◘ Do the majority of your employees subscribe to the organisation's vision and feel confident about its values, and are they keen to channel their commitment into productive activity for the organisation?

◘ What recent steps have been taken to promote a positive climate for learning in your organisation? What are the biggest barriers?

◘ Do managers and employees view the workplace as a learning environment? How widespread is this perception, and what degree of management commitment does it carry?

3 | Learning how to learn

The key is to see learning as inseparable from everyday work.

Peter Senge[1]

◻ Little in our evolution has prepared human beings for the demands of the modern workplace. This is why the development of learning capabilities ('learning how to learn') is such an important professional and life skill.

◻ Strategies for growing learning capabilities need to move beyond the training paradigm towards approaches that enable employees to take responsibility for their own learning and embed learning practices more systematically throughout the organisation.

◻ The shift from training to learning may be characterised as the progressive movement from the delivery of content to the development of learning capabilities as a people development strategy.

◻ Learning capabilities can be observed at three scales: the skills needed to manage one's own learning; those needed to harness the learning potential of groups; and the skills needed to catalyse organisational change.

◻ Becoming conscious of our learning decisions (ie when and how we practise learning behaviours), both individually and collectively, is an important step towards growing the range of capabilities in our repertoire.

Introduction

Although we are fortunate to be born with extensive learning capabilities, little in our evolution has prepared us for the demands of the modern workplace. This is why the progressive development of learning capabilities is such an important professional and life skill. Often described as 'learning how to learn', the challenge encompasses two related goals:

1 understanding clearly how the process of learning takes place, so that learning is approached in a systematic and disciplined fashion

2 understanding clearly how learning can be applied to organisational tasks, so that learning is more fully integrated with the process of work.

Learning capabilities can be developed at a range of scales, from mastery of personal development, to appreciation of group dynamics, and insight into the challenge of organisational change. Within the right climate for learning (see Chapter 2), learning capabilities enhance an organisation's ability to navigate future conditions – in short, they build adaptive capacity.

Although learning to learn is one of the most powerful and uniquely human capabilities, it remains a comparatively unexplored area of HRD practice. One explanation lies in the historic focus of the education sector on the teaching of subject-specific knowledge. From schools to universities, the skills of personal development, group dialogue and social change are given lower priority than the feeding of the intellect with data and information. The same pattern may be observed in organisations, where learning and content are often assumed to be the same thing.

Working outside the realms of education policy, HRD practitioners are better placed than many to challenge the fact-dominated culture of training that has permeated the education sector.

'…there is an urgent need to move beyond training as the dominant people-development paradigm.'

Developing awareness of the value of learning capabilities among employees, and facilitating greater discipline in their application to organisational tasks, should be an important goal for HR professionals.

Although we are starting from a low ebb, the potential pay-offs are significant. From senior management to the shop floor, an investment in learning capabilities represents an investment in the core adaptive strength of an organisation (its adaptive capacity). As Peter Honey and his colleagues in the Learning Declaration Group (2000) put it:

The ability to learn about learning and to harness the learning process is the key to our ability to survive in a complex and unpredictable world.

From training to learning

Given the need to prepare employees, teams and the overall culture of an organisation for a future of rapid and constant change, there is an urgent

need to move beyond training as the dominant people-development paradigm. Clearly, that does not imply the 'end' of training, or any such unlikely vision, but simply a stronger emphasis on supporting learning in the ways we know it actually occurs in practice.

> People believe they can only learn if they are in a classroom environment listening to a trainer delivering subject matter. They find it difficult to equate learning and development with everyday interactions during the normal work process.
> *Isobel Aitchison, Learning & Development Team Leader East, Glasgow Housing Association Ltd*

Before exploring the shift from training to learning, both terms must be clarified. For the purposes of this report, training will be characterised as an *instructor-led, content-based intervention*, leading to desired changes in behaviour, whereas learning

Figure 3 | The shift from training to learning

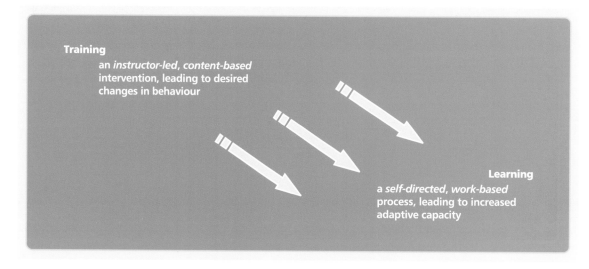

will be characterised as a *self-directed, work-based process*, leading to increased adaptive capacity (see Figure 3 on page 26). Clearly, this depiction of training is conventional in nature, and does not do justice to the wide range of training methods employed by practitioners. Nonetheless, while the difference is more modest than stated, there remains an important distinction between training and learning.

Following the above terminology, the shift from training to learning may be characterised as the *progressive movement from the delivery of content to the development of learning capabilities as a people development strategy*. Leading HRD practitioners have not been slow to pick up on this opportunity, which provides a direct link between the work of the training and development function and the strategic needs of the organisation. Table 3 (below) outlines some of the shift's key features.

Table 3 | Key features of training and learning

	Training	Learning
Responsibility	Organisation	Self or group
Process	Analysing needs, designing process, developing materials, delivering	Questioning, inventing, testing, reflecting
Approach	Expert- (or computer-)led instruction	Embedding learning practices in work
Defining relationship	Expert–novice	Peer–peer
Relevance to work	Variable, sometimes low	High (rooted in work challenges)
Transfer requirement	Yes	No
Impact	Brief, episodic	Ongoing, long-term
Style	Formal, planned	Informal, spontaneous
Benefits	Offers protected time for learning Signals organisational commitment	Integrates work and learning Builds adaptive capacity
Risks	Content is superseded, forgotten or remains unapplied	Learning is not aligned to organisation's strategic needs

> 'Helping employees to understand the learning process as something within their own control, rather than something that happens only in formal settings, is an important milestone in the transition.'

The shift is far easier to describe than to accomplish in practice, although the CIPD's research shows that many organisations are taking action to achieve the transition (CIPD 2004B). Efforts to encourage consistency, discipline and depth in the way that learning is practised across an organisation are bound to throw up cultural challenges, not least among HRD practitioners. And, of course, the support of two other groups in the organisation is vital: employees, the 'customers' for learning, and senior managers with significant influence over their behaviour. This suggests a two-pronged strategy:

1   Get employees on side, many of whom will retain conventional ideas about how learning takes place. Helping employees to understand the learning process as something within their own control, rather than something that happens only in formal settings, is an important milestone in the transition.

2   Get senior managers ('the business') on side, some of whom may not be conversant with the business case for learning. Familiarising them with the different levels at which learning can be practised, and the different tasks to which it can be applied, is a further milestone.

The background to these challenges is explored in the next two sections.

Understanding the learning process

One of the great advances in thinking about learning was its conceptualisation as a process rather than an outcome. The process involves a set of interlocking stages the learner passes through en route to increased competency, rather than the product of instruction. When understood as a process, in particular one that continues to unfold throughout life, it becomes clear that responsibility for learning rests with the individual. Although education and training can make important contributions along the way, ultimately learning is a self-directed process.

Several authors have depicted learning as a wheel, emphasising the continuous, cyclical nature of the process (egg Argyris 1982; Kolb 1984; Handy 1989; Engeström 2001). In Kolb's model, for example, **experience** is transformed, via **reflection**, into **theories** that guide future **activity**, and hence new experiences. While this is undoubtedly true, the model lacks clarity over what drives the learning process, in what direction it might be headed, and for what purpose.

Handy has addressed this issue by placing a **questioning** stage into the cycle, leading to a model similar to the one shown in Figure 4 (Handy 1989) on page 29. Here, learning begins with a sense of awareness (Argyris calls this 'discovery') of a problem or opportunity, out of which questions are born. This may be a choice between known alternatives ('My train is cancelled this morning: how shall I get to work?') or may enter less familiar territory ('My boss hasn't noticed a mistake in last month's budget: how shall I raise it?'). It may contain the seeds of a more complex investigation ('Our team is underachieving: how can we work together more productively?') or seek to challenge conventional wisdom ('Tom says our poor sales this quarter were due to manufacturing problems: could there be other explanations?').

Clearly these questions vary from the routine to the sophisticated. At the same time they share some common characteristics. A gap exists between where the person (or group) senses they ought to be and where they are currently, producing tensions that drive goal-seeking behaviours. The

Figure 4 I The wheel of learning (adapted from Handy, 1989)

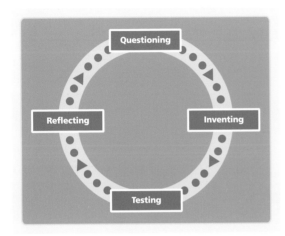

impetus to learn, act and adapt – to set the wheel in motion – originates through these tensions.

The remaining stages of the wheel offer a mechanism for addressing questions thrown up by the first stage. Briefly, the **inventing** stage (in Kolb's language 'abstract conceptualisation'; in Handy's 'theories') involves drawing on our existing understanding of the world in order to explain phenomena and envisage possible futures. The likely effects of different actions are rehearsed, out of which an hypothesis is formulated ('Based on what I know, doing x will achieve y'), leading to actions that take us closer to our goals.

Behind our hypotheses lie assumptions about how the world works, which may or may not be fully formed or correct. The **testing** stage of the wheel (Kolb's 'active experimentation'; Argyris's 'production') involves taking the actions we have formulated, thereby checking the validity of the hypothesis (the dilemmas present in real situations mean that our actions are rarely 100 per cent satisfactory).

Testing throws up 'data' on the strengths and weaknesses of our assumptions, and how they connect to other areas of knowledge. It gives rise to new experiences, not all of which will be expected or desired, or even fit within the range of possibilities predicted by our current models. Opportunities for **reflection** (Kolb's 'reflective observation'; Argyris's 'evaluation') follow, in which we update our assumptions about the world in order to explain why these experiences occurred. As Handy (1989, p. 48) says:

Change only sticks when we understand why it happened.

Reflection helps us to apply knowledge gained in one context to other situations we encounter – a process known as generalisation. When a child touches a hot radiator, it quickly realises that other radiators – large, small, short, tall – may provide a similar shock. It is not difficult to think of analogies in the workplace.

As we reflect upon the outcomes of our actions, new questions arise, and hence a new cycle of learning begins. Handy admits that the wheel is an idealised process that is 'difficult to start and hard to keep moving' (1989, p. 50), and that not all stages come naturally to every person – a fact that has been demonstrated by Peter Honey and Alan Mumford (1992; 2000) in their analysis of learning styles.

Applications of learning

Table 4 highlights four levels of learning that can be practised by employees and, by extension, groups of all kinds. Each level is associated with a different (and growing) set of learning capabilities and is suited to a different range of organisational applications. The levels form a spectrum, from

Table 4 | Levels of learning and their applications

	Hallmarks	Approach	Level of adaptation	Application
Level 0	React to events	Static	None	Routine tasks
Maintenance	Old approaches to new problems	Non-experimental	Goals and assumptions fixed	
Level 1	Respond to events	Deductive	Incremental	Short-term, tactical problems
Performance	Solve problems	Trial and error	Goals adapt, assumptions fixed	
Level 2	Understand events	Reflective	Deep	Medium-term, strategic challenges
Change	Reframe problems	Enquiring	Goals and assumptions adapt	
Level 3	Shape events	Generative	Continuous	Long-term, developmental goals
Agility	Anticipate problems	Learning as planning	Goals and assumptions fluid	

Adaptive capacity

'If there is an 'art' to learning, it is knowing which approach to apply at which time based on one's insight into the context and ramifications of the task at hand.'

non-adaptive behaviour (Level 0), sufficient to accomplish routine tasks, through to fully adaptive behaviour (Level 3), necessary when pursuing long-term developmental goals.[2]

Each higher level of learning implies:

◻ greater awareness (and mastery) of the learning process as it unfolds

◻ greater appreciation of the context in which learning is occurring

◻ a deeper process of questioning and reflection

◻ greater openness to adaptation, change and transformation

◻ a greater degree of conscious planning of the learning process

◻ greater need to involve others in the learning process.

The levels can be recognised in individuals and groups alike. We can talk about employee performance, change and agility just as easily as organisational performance, change and agility. The degree of growth felt by the learner (or learning group) increases from level to level, bringing greater flexibility of thought and action.

An analogy may be drawn with a vehicle following different, more sophisticated routes across a rough valley. At Level 0 it proceeds down a straight path until it collides with an obstacle and stops. At Level 1 it has enough flexibility to negotiate obstacles, explore alternative paths and keep moving towards its goal. At Level 2 the driver carries a map and can plan alternative, safer or shorter routes to the destination. At Level 3, the driver is thinking past

the immediate destination towards the next goal, and is fitting the vehicle with satellite navigation and all-terrain capability.

The levels of application are complementary rather than conflicting. Level 1 learning opens up new vistas for Level 0, Level 2 for Level 1, and so on. The point is that different situations call for different approaches to learning. If there is an 'art' to learning, it is knowing which approach to apply at which time based on one's insight into the context and ramifications of the task at hand. Becoming conscious of our learning decisions (ie when and how we practise learning behaviours), both individually and collectively, is an important step towards recognising and growing the range of capabilities in our repertoire.

Identifying learning capabilities

> There is a need to educate people about how and when they go about learning, and at present we do not do this.
> *Des Woods, Head of Learning and Organisational Development, Linklaters*

Figure 5 on page 32 illustrates how learning capabilities may be interpreted as the 'oil' that lubricates the learning wheel, bringing forward its stages of questioning, inventing, testing and reflecting. Clearly, it is impossible to reduce learning to a single behaviour, since it flows from the combination of behaviours necessary to accomplish all stages of the wheel. When they are present, individually or collectively, the wheel will turn, leading not only to new knowledge and skills, but also to questions answered, problems solved and improvements made.

Figure 5 | Oiling the learning wheel

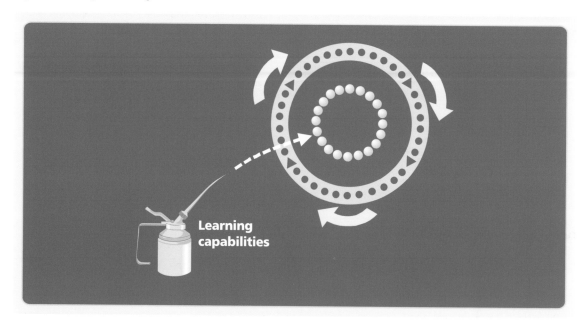

**Learning
capabilities**

The transition to learning depends on cultivating learning capabilities, yet this task does not fall into any neat subject area or well-developed theoretical box. With little to anchor the analysis, other than an agreed definition and process for learning, it seems sensible to break the task down according to the unit of study: people, groups and organisations. While the adaptive capacity of an organisation depends on learning at all three scales, each will be associated with a unique set of learning capabilities.

Individual capabilities

Many of the learning capabilities brought to work by employees have been acquired in other contexts, such as childhood, social activities, educational experiences, parenting and other life phases. The ability to construct relationships, involve others in tasks, frame and reframe

problems, plan activities, sift information, set goals and find solutions are examples. Other learning skills, like exploring scenarios, engaging in dialogue with colleagues, and reflecting on work outcomes, require a more disciplined and collaborative approach to learning and may need to be developed directly by the organisation.

The challenge for those wishing to develop individual learning capabilities is to view the workplace as a 'learning laboratory' where skills are refined over a period of time in response to (and to the advantage of) work activities. In the right climate, every work task can be conceptualised as an opportunity to learn at one or more of the levels identified in Table 4. That is not to say that the discipline of learning is something that can be acquired overnight, even by the brightest, most committed people. But with increasing confidence and, as necessary, specialist learning support (see Chapter 4), every employee should be encouraged to practise learning at the higher levels.

> Some people don't like to think at times, and would rather be told what to do in case anything goes wrong.
> *Isobel Aitchison, Learning & Development Team Leader East, Glasgow Housing Association Ltd*

Two caveats: confidence and ability

1   The capacity to direct one's own learning is critical for self-development. Yet not all employees possess the confidence to take on this role. Lack of confidence tends to narrow horizons and curtail expectations, with the effect that learning opportunities are missed and potential remains unfulfilled. Achievement is replaced by a sense of 'muddling through' as old tactics are applied to new problems. Careful development coaching and planning – taking into account the person in their whole context, not just their role as an employee – can build confidence and, with it, the desire to learn.

> The right environment can bring out the best in all people. But should we also recognise that some individuals are going to benefit more than others? Not all plants have the same propensity to grow.
> *Geoff Pye, Consultant, Genie Partnership*

2   Individual ability (itself a product of numerous factors such as background, intelligence, experience, relationships etc) is one of the

many factors influencing learning. It should not be overplayed, however, as there is evidence to suggest that employees without any obvious gift or talent can exhibit strong performance when their motivation is nurtured by the organisation (O'Reilly and Pfeffer 2000). Nonetheless, ability will have an impact on learning – within any defined time period and situation, every person has a ceiling on their potential.

Group capabilities

Group behaviour has an overwhelming impact on organisational life, not least because the majority of work is experienced through group activity. From boards to social clubs, the effect of group decisions on employees is real and pervasive, including their learning. By clarifying group intentions, the decision-making process forms a bridge between the group's vision and individual, goal-led action, creating torque to turn the learning wheel.

Decisions made in a group setting, if allowed to arise without manipulation or coercion, can result in a powerful and sustained commitment to action. In a paper published shortly after his death, Kurt Lewin explained this phenomenon as follows (Gold 1999, p. 273):

One of the reasons why 'group-carried changes' are more readily brought about seems to be the unwillingness of the individual to depart too far from group standards; he is likely to change only if the group changes.

A successful group is able to clarify its situation, understand its resources, act on its problems, take advantage of its opportunities and learn from its experiences. Underpinning its success are people

> '...there is a world of difference between talking about learning and ensuring that it is promoted in practice.'

who are able to view problems as collective endeavours rather than individual pursuits. People who are disciplined in using dialogue;[3] skilful in generating and sharing knowledge to the group's advantage; sensitive to each other's needs; and honest in their approach to gaining group commitment. These are the learning capabilities most vital to group functioning.

Group dynamics are complicated, and employees may lack the skills and knowledge to make them work. As a result, few groups could claim to operate without some degree of dysfunction. Irving Janis (1984) referred to this as 'group think' or 'group norms that bolster morale at the expense of critical thinking' (p. 167):

One of the most common norms appears to be that of remaining loyal to the group by sticking with the policies to which the group has already committed itself, even when those policies are obviously working out badly and have unintended consequences that disturb the conscience of each member.

Group dynamics have a significant impact on learning in organisations, both positive and negative. On the one hand, group decisions can drive the learning process by sealing commitment to an ambitious goal. On the other, group dysfunction can bring learning to a standstill by fixing people to unhealthy norms. Educating employees about the opportunities and pitfalls of group dynamics is probably the most significant thing an organisation can do to increase its capacity to learn.

Organisational capabilities

Most (if not all) organisations would profess their support for learning. The word sits alongside other organisational mantras like 'innovation', 'quality' and 'competitive advantage', having reached iconic status in management literature. While this is a positive sign, there is a world of difference between talking about learning and ensuring that it is promoted in practice. The hallmarks of a learning culture are empowerment over supervision; self-managed learning over instruction; long-term capacity-building over short-term fixes. In this respect, many organisations are not nearly as successful as their rhetoric may imply.

Brakes on learning are revealed most clearly during periods of change, when the seeds of new strategies are searching for a niche in which to grow. Resistance can appear in several guises: suspicion of the change vision (the 'them and us' phenomenon); confusion, due to poor communication of vision; lack of confidence (or capacity) to adopt new practices; inertia within established power bases; systems that are misaligned with the vision; and a lack of learning capabilities at the individual or group scales. As Lewin said, 'You cannot understand a system until you try to change it' (Marrow 1969).

> Traditional learning is stuck in high-direction, low-support mode.
> *Peter Fonseca, OD Manager,*
> *Stanley Europe*

Not all models of change are equally susceptible to such problems. Certainly, large-scale initiatives, driven by managers at the top or centre of an organisation, can create upheaval, confusion, even fear, as they unfold. Typically, these initiatives conceptualise change as a short, sharp, episodic process, done to the organisation for its own benefit: downsizing and re-engineering projects are common examples. Change initiatives of this kind can be costly and prone to failure: it is extremely hard to generate ownership of a change process among people who are not involved in its planning, do not understand why it is necessary and cannot see any individual benefit, no matter how much 'support' they are given by the initiators.

For this reason, the approach is gradually giving way to one that conceptualises change as a continuous, emergent phenomenon – a process of 'changing' rather than change (Wick and Quinn 1999). The core assumption of this new model is that organisations cannot be directed, only 'disturbed', with change arising as employees make sense of the disturbance (Higgs and Rowland 2003). Ongoing research from CIPD has confirmed the validity of this perspective (CIPD 2003C).

The impetus for learning can arise anywhere in an organisation, not only from managers at the top or centre.[4] Employees in outward-facing roles who detect changes in customer requirements, or who are exposed to learning opportunities among suppliers and partners, may feel the disturbance most keenly; engineers and specialists who encounter difficulties with processes or technologies may be the first to prompt improvements. The assumption is that change is grounded in local improvements of work practices, rather than centralised strategic ideas. Small adjustments, occurring simultaneously in many places, then accumulate into larger organisational impacts (Wick and Quinn 1999). As Sather and Davidson (2000, p.295) put it:

The goal is to eliminate the necessity of unfreezing the organization in future by retaining enough fluidity in most aspects of the organization's culture that 'moving' will be simply a matter of changing speed or course.

Summary

This chapter began by noting the role of learning capabilities in preparing employees for the demands of the modern workplace. The discussion highlighted the need to move beyond the training paradigm towards approaches that enable employees to take responsibility for their own learning, and embed learning practices more systematically within their work and throughout the organisation.

In leading the shift from training to learning, the challenge for the HR function is to gain the endorsement of both the majority of employees and the organisation's senior managers. A key message to employees is that the learning process is something within their own sphere of influence, rather than something that happens only in formal settings. A key message to senior managers is that learning is supported by a solid business case, practising what you preach, and has numerous business applications.

In order to grow learning capabilities, you need to be able to define them. The discussion offered a preliminary description of the capabilities needed to manage one's own learning; those needed to harness the learning potential of groups; and the skills needed to catalyse organisational change. The second step is to bring discipline to the learning process, by surfacing our understanding of how and when we practise learning behaviours, both individually and collectively. Only then can the capabilities become embedded in the organisation.

Inevitably, strategies for growing learning capabilities will seek to expose employees to a richer and more powerful set of learning processes than they would normally encounter during work. The design of *learning interventions* forms the subject of the final chapter of this report.

> We need to move away from intervention-centred development towards a learning culture.
>
> *Jane Sloan, Training Manager, ITV plc*

Endnotes

1   Senge (1999, p. 24).

2   The approach casts Bateson's (2000) analysis in organisational terms, drawing also on Argyris and Schön's (1978) distinction between single- and double-loop learning. For completeness, Bateson (2000, p. 293) identified a fifth level of learning that incorporates an evolutionary element but concluded that it 'probably does not occur in any adult living organism on this earth'.

3   For a superlative discussion of dialogue see Isaacs (1999).

4   Although there remains much that these groups can do to recognise, support and communicate emergent change as it occurs for the benefit of others in the organisation.

Questions for your organisation

◘   Is the distinction between training and learning well recognised in your organisation, or do managers and employees equate the two? Are you taking any steps to reinforce the distinction?

◘   Are the benefits of 'learning how to learn' well understood by your department? If so, what recent steps have you taken to build learning capabilities in your organisation, and what processes were involved?

◘   Are your managers and employees aware of the power of groups to unlock or constrain learning? How effectively do groups operate? Are you doing anything to improve their understanding of group dynamics?

4 | Learning interventions

The old model of education, going back to classical times, dealt only with the education of the intellect, theoretical and applied. The new model integrates this with emotional, interpersonal and political competence. Nowadays we have people who are learning by thinking, feeling and doing – bringing all these to bear on the acquisition of new knowledge and skills.

John Heron[1]

◻ Learning interventions have the potential to help employees deepen their learning capabilities, allowing them to take greater responsibility (individually or collectively) for their own learning.

◻ Not all intervention methods encourage self-directed learning. Those that rely too heavily on external expertise or content, rather than paying attention to the needs of the learner in their work context, fall into this category.

◻ Managers and HRD professionals can grow learning capabilities most effectively by fulfilling roles that engage the learner in a discussion about their own situation and challenges, letting them decide what actions they wish to initiate.

◻ The results of the CIPD's annual training and development survey suggest that HRD practitioners are using techniques such as coaching and action learning to devolve responsibility for learning to managers and employees.

◻ While training remains an effective means of facilitating learning in certain areas of people development practice, there remain many opportunities to improve the design of training interventions.

Introduction

In preceding chapters we have noted the value of two complementary ways to promote learning in organisations. Firstly, the creation of a positive climate for learning (a 'growth medium'), which is predominantly an issue of management action and style (Chapter 2). Secondly, the development of learning capabilities among employees (their 'learning to learn' skills), a challenge that is shared between managers and HRD practitioners (Chapter 3). Taken together, these two approaches offer a powerful way to build the adaptive capacity of an organisation.

Both approaches can be facilitated by interventions designed to bring insight and discipline to the learning process. At the same time, they can also be disrupted by interventions that do not focus sufficiently on the day-to-day experiences of the learner (or learning group). As many of us can attest, sitting through a presentation about matters related only weakly to our situation is not a helpful experience.

The fact is that no one understands the work context and learning needs of a person better than themselves, making it practically impossible to design content of generic appeal. By implication, many of an organisation's key development needs will always remain unsupported by training, not least because they are difficult to define, are specific to the organisation's context and are subject to rapid fluctuations.

Engeström (2001, p. 139) sums up the collective realisation of a group of Finnish health-care workers who are grappling with a series of deep flaws in their patient care model:

There was no readily available model that would fix the problems. No wise teacher had the correct answer.

> 'The problem is that self-directed learning is a fragile commodity in organisations and needs to be carefully nurtured.'

Certainly this form of realisation will cause alarm for some, but for many it will be deeply empowering. Freed from the tyranny of content-based solutions, intervention designers can get down to the more pressing task of designing *learning interventions* for employees, ie interventions that deepen the learning capabilities of employees, helping them to progress (individually or collectively) their own agenda.

The challenge of self-direction

Until employees (and the groups in which they participate) learn to master the processes necessary to further their own learning, they will be forever dependent on external guidance and support. The problem is that self-directed learning is a fragile commodity in organisations and needs to be carefully nurtured. It can be easily damaged by interventions that are too directive in nature or too focused on expert input, rather than the knowledge and needs of the participants.

> Considerable learning takes place in unplanned ways as part of everyday life, though this is not always as effective or as positive as it might be. This is why organisations take deliberate actions to provide efficient and effective ways to support purposeful learning.
> *Graham O'Connell, CMPS, Cabinet Office*

This presents a major challenge for HRD professionals, but also a major opportunity. In the same way that managerial role models help to create a positive climate for learning, HRD practitioners can lead the development of new models of intervention design. Role models lead by example, tapping into the human instinct to try

out positive behaviours observed in other people. The methods used in learning interventions should therefore be transparent to the participants. This may involve an explicit effort on the part of the intervention team to explain how the learning process is designed to work.

Participants should leave an intervention feeling confident that they can apply the same methods in their own domain. As Argyris (1982, p. 161) notes, methods of intervention that follow the natural process of learning (ie questioning, inventing, testing, reflecting, questioning…) strengthen the participants' ability to replicate them at a later date:

*As the participants reflect on how they learn…
they will be learning how they would learn for any
similar problem.*

At a more practical level, intervention specialist John Heron stresses the need to obtain clarity on the intentions and purposes of an intervention before tackling the detailed design (Heron 2001). He provides a rich framework for the intervention designer, tracing broad intentions all the way through to specific activities and facilitation techniques. It is worth observing that Heron attaches particular significance to the 'catalytic' form of intervention that 'seeks to elicit self-discovery, self-directed living, learning and problem-solving in the client' (p. 6).

Management and HRD roles

Table 5, opposite, identifies a series of roles for managers and HRD professionals, designed to support the growth of learning capabilities. The roles are analysed in terms of the scale at which they apply (individual, group, organisation), and the levels of learning they seek to promote (see Table 4 on page 30). This table builds on the analysis presented in Chapters 2 and 3.

Table 5 | Management and HRD roles in building learning capabilities

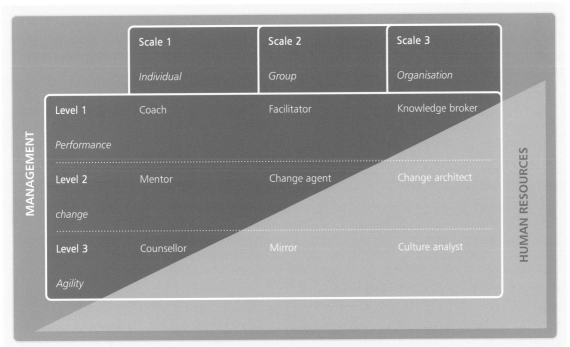

	Scale 1 *Individual*	Scale 2 *Group*	Scale 3 *Organisation*
Level 1 *Performance*	Coach	Facilitator	Knowledge broker
Level 2 *change*	Mentor	Change agent	Change architect
Level 3 *Agility*	Counsellor	Mirror	Culture analyst

There is no universal agreement on the definitions of the roles. The descriptions below are those adopted by the author. For a fuller discussion of many of these roles, see the CIPD Guide, *Coaching and Buying Coaching Services* (CIPD 2004A).

Each role is designed to encourage self-responsibility for the learning process. Hence the role of a facilitator is to help a group make sense of its situation and arrive at collective decisions, not to advocate specific actions. The purpose of a change architect is to grow organisational structures that will catalyse change, not to over-ride local initiatives with top-down solutions. This point may sound pedantic, even perverse. Why not be more directive? Yet it is crucial that the roles grow generic learning capabilities as well as attending to current priorities.

Individual development

◘ Coach. This role aims to boost performance by helping the learner to unpack challenges, think through options, reflect on outcomes and progress towards work practices that deliver the organisation's vision. The role of the coach is to listen, clarify and explore, rather than instruct, direct or subdue, ceding responsibility for decisions to the learner to the maximum extent, unless specifically requested otherwise.

◘ Mentor. This role has different aims from those of coaching. The mentor steps back from day-to-day performance issues to focus on the context in which the learner is operating. This provides an opportunity to explore how the learner's work relates to the organisation's strategic objectives; how those objectives are likely to evolve over time; and how the learner might need to adjust their approach and capabilities to enhance their contribution. The mentor provides an intimate *practice field* in which new insights can be generated without disruption to immediate work activities. The techniques of first person action inquiry, dialogue and critical reflection are practised to strengthen the learner's ability to identify, analyse and respond to change as it arises.

> We recognise that the learner-centred approach will fail without good support processes, so the key for us is to move our culture away from traditional line management to facilitative management, where managers encourage people to take responsibility for their own learning and development. This requires coaches and mentors rather than supervisors, something we have now accepted as a key to our future success.
>
> *Andy Cooke, Coaching and Mentoring Consultant for Shell EP*

◘ Counsellor. People develop assumptions about what works based upon their own experience. When they face a situation where their traditional approaches do not work (maybe because the environment has changed), some people find it difficult to see beyond their existing assumptions and values. In such cases they may be too embarrassed to own up to their own vulnerability or uncertainty (words that are often associated with profound learning), forming a block on their future development. The role of the counsellor is to help the person make their assumptions explicit, so that they can be discussed, tested and, if necessary, changed. Traditional development planning focuses on the skills and knowledge required by the organisation as it is currently framed, whereas the counsellor also explores the long-term development of the person. The aim is to prepare the person for probable but unknowable futures by developing their generic learning capabilities. In this way their contribution to the organisation can be optimised.

Group development

◘ Facilitator. This role aims to create an atmosphere in which a group can clarify its goals, review its options, and formulate its approach to common challenges – in short, meet its own needs. The facilitator must resist the temptation to influence the group's thinking on a topic: their role is to harness and focus energy in the group, not to manipulate its thinking – in other words, to catalyse the potential of the group. Success is measured in terms of the group's ability to meet its goals efficiently and effectively.

> The best interventions act as catalysts to the learning process. They provide the chance to be different, to let go of blocks, to unlearn some of our deepest habits.
>
> *Roger Bellis, Rowland Fisher Lexon Consultancy*

◘ Change agent. This role aims to 'unfreeze' the conventional logic of the group so that it can restore its energy and let go of its blocks. Although confrontation may be appropriate in some instances, the change agent achieves results primarily through collaborative reflection and enquiry. The role differs from facilitation: where the latter seeks efficiency, the change agent seeks to check and, if need be, challenge the validity of conventional practices. This is achieved by stepping back from immediate tasks in order to question goals, explore assumptions, surface values and achieve a greater awareness of how the group is contributing to the organisation, how it is perceived by other groups and how healthily it is functioning internally. The change agent creates a practice field in which new realities can be discussed and new approaches piloted. In this way systemic problems in the group's operation can be avoided and its contribution to the organisation can be greatly enhanced.

> The most successful interventions occur when participants can see a direct link between the intervention and their own working environment.
> *David Jones, Manager Group Learning Services, HSBC Learning and Development*

◘ Mirror. Most groups present a variety of dysfunctions in their operation. Some cannot achieve clarity of purpose; others are unable to practise effective dialogue; some operate long after their sell-by date, immune to their diminished contribution; others contain members with entrenched positions or members who are irrationally loyal to the group's commitments; yet others hide behind defensive conversational routines rather than looking inwards for the solution to organisational problems (Argyris 1991; 1993). The first role of anyone trying to help the group is to hold up a mirror such that it can view its own behaviour with some degree of dignity and objectivity. The second is to work with the group to strengthen its learning capabilities. Typical aims are to replace argument with dialogue, insularity with openness, defensiveness with enquiry, assumption with reflection, blame with support, and power with respect – developments that add value across numerous task domains.

Organisational development

◘ Knowledge communicator/broker. This role aims to spread news of key events, opportunities and threats in the external environment (for example, stakeholder perceptions and trends) to ensure that employees are aware of the most relevant sources of influence on their work. Crucially, the role also involves conveying stories and practical examples of how work is being adjusted across the organisation, including how problems are being reframed. In large organisations, where the detail of the stories may be remote or inaccessible, a brokerage service should be established to build ties between people with relevant experience to share. The role not only helps to recognise and replicate best practice but to establish connections of ongoing value between employees.

◘ Change architect. This role aims to accelerate change in the parts of the organisation where it is most needed. The role works by creating the conditions (the practice field) in which pilot projects, experiments and processes of enquiry can be conducted to gain insight into work activities and commitment to new practices. The role should be facilitative rather than instrumental: while recognising the importance of a clear and replicable learning process, change should be allowed to emerge from the

'...the majority of HRD professionals believe that the responsibility for learning
and development lies firmly within *their* domain...'

groups affected without direction or coercion. Cross-functional working groups, inter-departmental task forces, inter-organisation learning forums and partnerships with academic units all provide potential structures on which to base appreciative and collaborative enquiry.

◘ Culture analyst. This role aims to assess the cultural obstacles to change in an organisation and advise employees (in particular managers and HRD practitioners) on where to focus their change efforts. The challenge of cultural change is like an iceberg: the visible part represents the events, behaviours and experiences encountered in daily work; below this lies the espoused values and beliefs of employees – the things they claim as valuable, the official reasons they give for behaving as they do; lower down are the core assumptions on which actions are really based, often so ingrained that few people are aware of them (Roth and Kleiner 2000). Fundamental change depends on understanding why current situations have arisen as much as on planning

how they might be altered in future. The role of the culture analyst is to work with groups to surface core assumptions and demonstrate how they influence the progress of the organisation. While self-assessment tools and surveys of organisational climate are useful, the key tool in the culture analyst's box is group dialogue.

What's happening in practice?

Every year, the CIPD carries out a survey of the state of training and development practice in the UK. The survey provides a useful barometer of opinion from a wide range of practitioners, permitting changes in perspective and underlying trends to be identified. The 2004 survey provides evidence that the shift from training to learning is underway in the UK but still has a considerable distance to go (CIPD 2004B).

Figure 6, below, illustrates how HRD professionals responded when asked who they thought had the main responsibility for driving learning and development activity.

Figure 6 | Perceptions of responsibility for learning and development

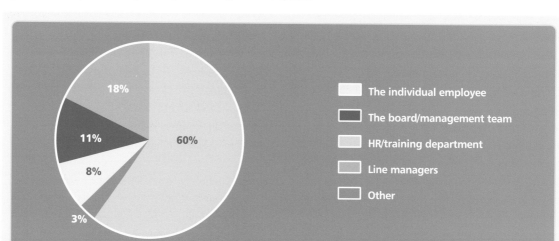

> '**Fundamentally, the shift to learning depends on distributing responsibility for learning to the maximum extent possible...**'

This telling picture suggests that the majority of HRD professionals believe that the responsibility for learning and development lies firmly within *their* domain, with a much smaller role interpreted as belonging to line managers and individual employees. This form of response is consistent with the view of the profession as an instrumental force in learning. However, it does suggest a rather unbalanced concentration of responsibility for learning among corporate specialists and a lack of awareness of the value of self-directed learning among managers and employees. This is especially true given their recognition of the importance and effectiveness of informal learning.

Given the preceding discussions, two questions immediately arise:

◻ If the climate for learning was stronger in the 500 organisations surveyed, would employees be inspired to take greater responsibility for their own learning?

◻ If the learning capabilities of managers and employees were enhanced, would they begin to rely less on external direction?

Fundamentally, the shift to learning depends on distributing responsibility for learning to the maximum extent possible, out of specialist departments and into line management roles, operational functions, team leaders and individual employees. This does not mean downing tools within HRD but, instead, focusing on creating a growth medium for learning across the organisation, and building learning capabilities.

Here the picture is much more positive. When asked whether line managers should play a significant role in helping their teams to learn and develop, a total of 94 per cent of those surveyed

agreed. Similarly, when asked whether employees should take more responsibility for their own learning and development, 92 per cent agreed. This suggests that HRD practitioners are not comfortable with the present picture, and are eager, although not necessarily equipped, to devolve responsibilities for learning to managers and staff.

In terms of the techniques used by HRD practitioners to achieve their aims, the survey revealed some very interesting trends. Figure 7, on page 44, illustrates how people responded when asked whether they had increased or decreased the use of specific development techniques over the last year.

The results indicate a significant increase in coaching and mentoring practices, which is highly consistent with the roles identified in Table 4. Assuming that managers play at least some role in the provision of the coaching and mentoring, this finding provides further evidence that responsibilities for learning are being devolved in organisations.

It is interesting to note the growth of other areas, like job rotation, secondment and shadowing, that provide opportunities for employees to immerse themselves in the experience of other people's work. Techniques of the kind can create powerful learning experiences, as well as such implicit benefits as building new connections and relationships, exposure to role models and awareness of different management styles.

A further technique showing a significant increase in 2004 is action learning. Pioneered by Reg Revans in the years following the Second World War, action learning has proved to be one of the most effective frameworks for learning yet invented (see

> '...training has an important complementary role to play in accelerating learning, alongside these other, less directive strategies.'

Figure 7 | Net increases in the use of specific training and development techniques

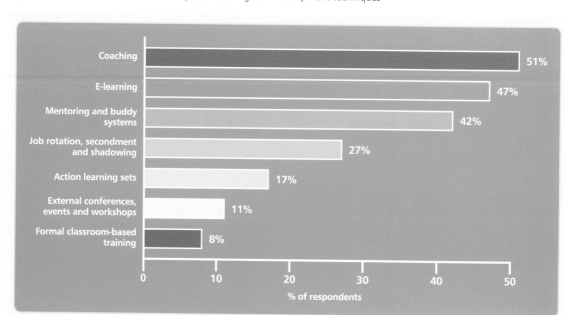

Bushy 2000 for examples). Action learning has always lived in the shadow of conventional 'show and tell' training yet, being rooted in the (often humble) reality of work-based challenges, it epitomises the shift from training to learning.

E-learning also shows a large increase in 2004, although the diversity of techniques falling under this label makes this result hard to interpret in methodological terms. E-learning is, after all, a channel rather than a technique. In time it could, if properly managed, prove to be a powerful means to support devolved learning.

Where does training fit in?

The roles outlined earlier in this chapter draw heavily on interventions – even individual interactions such as coaching and mentoring can be recognised as a form of intervention. The remainder of this chapter explores the role of a specific type of intervention not included in the previous discussion, ie training. The reason training was not included in Table 5 is that, in its conventional form, it does not seek explicitly to develop learning capabilities (see Table 3).

By now, you could be forgiven for concluding that the gist of this report is that training is at best a peripheral process to learning, at worst a destructive procedure, given its capacity to breed dependency on external direction and expertise. After all, if the majority of learning occurs through the experience of work and is influenced by organisational culture, climate and learning capabilities, why bother with training at all?

The answer is that training has an important complementary role to play in accelerating learning, alongside these other, less directive

> '...a course is simply a period of dedicated learning time that may be used in whatever way necessary to promote the development of its participants.'

strategies. If this report does have a position on training, it is simply to suggest that training is reserved for situations that justify a more directed, expert-led approach, rather than viewing it as a comprehensive and all-pervasive people-development solution.

Three situations where training is fully justified are described below:

◘ When critical information must be imparted to employees to ensure they meet their responsibilities. Health and safety concerns, legal compliance and essential competencies shared by large groups of people (for example, operating a till in a retail outlet) fall into this category. The required skills could be picked up by on-the-job observation of colleagues, trial and error, and coaching, but this won't necessarily occur with the speed or certainty demanded by the task.

◘ When challenges are so specialised or complex that employees are unlikely to master them on their own initiative, at least not at an appropriate speed. The use of specialised software, procedures and work-flow processes fall into this category. A great deal of information needs to be imparted and procedures checked and double-checked to ensure they are robustly understood. Time with an expert instructor can act as a useful complement to self-study or group-development processes, substantially speeding up the appearance of new skills.

◘ When the subject material is so generic that the learner has no difficulty in relating it to their own context. Staff induction

programmes, essential IT skills, time management and presentation skills all fit this description, since the same stories, examples and group processes are suitable for practically everyone. That is not to say that the instructor should be blind to individual differences in learning style, prior knowledge and learning confidence, or to the specific work challenges of those involved. The basic challenge, however, is to acknowledge such differences while attempting to pull everyone up to the same level, after which individuals can specialise in accordance with the demands of their roles.

Having noted three areas that justify training (the critical, the specialised and the generic), the issue becomes how to make sure the training is effective. It is important to appreciate that a course is simply a period of dedicated learning time that may be used in whatever way necessary to promote the development of its participants. There is nothing in the name to suggest that it must be instructor-led, be wholly content-based or, indeed, follow any other design philosophy. Many courses place greater emphasis on process than content, and some even place the design of the process into the hands of the participants.

This design process begins with an in-depth understanding of the learner in their work context. Events are planned only where specific value can be added compared with informal, work-based learning opportunities, which suggests the need to involve managers in most stages of the process, including post-training evaluation. Table 6, on page 46, contains a variety of practical suggestions to help training practitioners boost the effectiveness of their interventions and follow-up processes.

Table 6 | Practical suggestions for effective training

1 Take time to discuss the rationale behind the training carefully, including how it supports group and organisational goals. Engage line managers in this discussion.

2 Establish a positive learning atmosphere by ensuring everyone has a chance to introduce themselves and contribute to discussions without fear or intimidation.

3 Be transparent about the training methods used, explaining why they were chosen, what capabilities they are intended to build and how they can be applied to ongoing work.

4 Draw extensively on the knowledge and experience of the participants.

5 Recognise the power of collaborative learning. Encourage reflection, enquiry, dialogue and debate.

6 Don't overload participants with information: if technical information is required provide a list of pre-reading or websites to browse.

7 Relate the subject material of the training to the work contexts of the participants. Ideally, make their work a central feature of the content.

8 Explore the dilemmas present in real situations, as well as distant or artificial cases.

9 Encourage participants to enquire into all aspects of their current and prospective roles: What can we learn from the past? What can we improve now? How can we redesign things for the future?

10 Help form connections among the participants that will be of long-term value to their work.

11 Extend the reach of the learning process before and after individual events, taking opportunities to embed learning in work.

12 Use technology to help to provide channels for ongoing learning and communication.

Although they are designed to improve specific knowledge or skills, training interventions also contain other, implicit opportunities for learning. For example, good training will use the opportunity of the group's presence to develop their learning capabilities. Conscious use (and explanation) of methods such as group dialogue, storytelling, critical reflection and action inquiry, if appropriate to the topic area, can enrich the training experience while equipping the participants with powerful new skill-sets to apply in their own work. Above all, training can act as a breeding ground for new relationships, connections and ideas, simulating the informal learning processes that are so effective (but under-recognised) in work.

> Courses often help employees to 'open up', but structuring them in a way that encourages employees to put their 'development achievements' into practice back in the workplace presents a major design challenge.
> *Des Woods, Head of Learning and Organisational Development, Linklaters*

We all know what an effective training process feels like. It inspires us to go out and get to grips with an issue ourselves rather than wait for authoritative instructions. Bringing people together to receive information from experts is not sufficient as a training process – the participants can do this on their own through books and websites.

> I for one try to find interesting ways to get participants to discuss, experience and learn from training, rather than just provide information. The downside is that this takes longer, and in today's bite-sized training events it isn't easy to achieve.
> *Roger Pattison, Consultant, Roger Pattison & Assoviates*

Summary

This chapter began by noting the potential of interventions to help employees deepen their

learning capabilities, allowing them to take greater responsibility (individually or collectively) for their own learning. It also noted the potential of some types of intervention to disrupt self-directed learning by paying insufficient attention to the needs of the learner in their work context.

Methods that rely heavily on the transfer of external expertise or content to employees were observed to carry the highest risk in this regard, since their design is often removed from the context in which work is created. As a result it is impossible to meet learning needs adequately. The discussion concluded that the most practical solution to the design of learning interventions is to step back from the course-production treadmill in order to explore more directly how to help employees (and the groups in which they operate) take charge of their own learning agenda.

A number of specific roles for managers and HRD professionals were proposed. Working at different scales and learning levels, each role aims to engage the learner in a discussion about their own situation and challenges, while letting them decide what actions they wish to initiate. A common ethos of true helping behaviour, unburdened by the desire to influence or control, permeates each role.

The results of the CIPD's recent training and development survey indicate that HRD practitioners are eager, although not necessarily fully equipped, to support the move to self-directed learning. The results show that they are promoting techniques like coaching and action learning to devolve responsibility for learning to managers and employees.

The final section of the chapter explored the important and complementary role of training in promoting learning in organisations. While

'**Without doubt, the experience of work always will provide the richest learning laboratory.**'

training remains the most obvious (and cost-effective) method in several specialist areas of people development, there remain many opportunities to improve the design of training interventions. Without doubt, the experience of work always will provide the richest learning laboratory.

Endnote

1   Heron (2001, p. 208).

Questions for your organisation

- Are your employees confident about directing their own learning? Does this apply consistently across different levels and parts of the organisation?

- Do your HRD professionals possess the skills necessary to fulfil the roles involved in developing learning capabilities at individual, group and organisational levels?

- Where do your interventions sit on the spectrum from training to learning? Are they vehicles for delivering content, or do they encourage participants to take charge of their own learning?

- Are you making the shift from training to learning, and how can you accelerate progress?

References

ARGYRIS, C. (1977)

'Double loop learning in organizations'. *Harvard Business Review*, September–October 1977.

ARGYRIS, C. (1982)

Reasoning, Learning, and Action: individual and organizational. San Francisco: Jossey-Bass.

ARGYRIS, C. (1990)

Integrating the Individual and the Organization. New Brunswick: Transaction Publishers.

ARGYRIS, C. (1991)

'Teaching smart people how to learn'. *Harvard Business Review*. May–June 1991.

ARGYRIS, C. (1993)

Knowledge for Action: a guide to overcoming barriers to organisational change. San Francisco: Bass-Bass Publishers.

ARGYRIS, C. AND SCHÖN, D.A. (1978)

Organization Learning: a theory of action perspective. Reading, MA: Addison-Wesley.

ASHKANASY, N.M., WILDEROM, C.P.M. AND PETERSON, M.F. (2000)

Handbook of Organizational Culture and Climate. Thousand Oaks, CA: Sage Publications.

BANDURA, A. (1977)

Social Learning Theory. Englewood Cliffs, NJ: Prentice Hall.

BATESON, G. (2000) [1972]

Steps to an Ecology of Mind. Chicago: University of Chicago Press.

BUSHY, Y. (ED.) (2000)

Business Driven Action Learning: global best practices. London: Macmillan Business.

BROWN, J.S. AND DUGUID, P. (1991)

Organizational learning and communities of practice: toward a unified view of working, learning, and innovation. *Organization Science*. 2: 40–57.

CALEY, L. AND REID, S. (2003)

Key Influencing Factors of Work-related Learning. NHS Modernization Agency, Leadership Centre.

CAPLAN, J. (2003)

Coaching for the Future: how smart companies use coaching and mentoring. London: Chartered Institute of Personnel and Development.

CIPD (2002)A

Pressure of Work and the Psychological Contract. Research Report. London: The Chartered Institute of Personnel and Development.

CIPD (2002)B

How do People Learn? Research Report. London: Chartered Institute of Personnel and Development.

CIPD (2003)A

Focus on the Learner. Change Agenda. London: Chartered Institute of Personnel and Development.

CIPD (2003)B

Bringing Policies to Life: the role of front line managers. Executive Briefing. London: Chartered Institute of Personnel and Development.

CIPD (2003)C

Organising for Success in the Twenty-First Century. Research Report. London: Chartered Institute of Personnel and Development.

CIPD (2003)D

Understanding the People and Performance Link: unlocking the black box. London: Chartered Institute of Personnel and Development.

CIPD (2004)A

Coaching and Buying Coaching Services: a guide. London: Chartered Institute of Personnel and Development.

CIPD (2004)B

Training and Development 2004: survey report. London: Chartered Institute of Personnel and Development.

COLLINS, J., THOMAS, G., WILLIS, R. AND WILSON, J. (2003)

Carrots, Sticks and Sermons: influencing public behaviour for environmental goals. Report prepared for Defra. Demos/Green Alliance, London.

CUNNINGHAM, I. (2004)

'Back to reality?' *People Management*. 8 April 2004.

DEMING, W.E. (1992)

Dr Deming's Four Day Seminar. Recorded at General Motors, July 1992. See http://www.deming.org.

ENGESTRÖM, Y. (2001)

'Expansive learning at work: toward an activity theoretical reconceptualisation'. *Journal of Education and Work*. Vol. 14, No. 1.

ENOS, M.D., KEHRHAHN, M.T. AND BELL, A. (2003)

'Informal learning and the transfer of learning: how managers develop proficiency'. *Human Resource Development Quarterly*. Vol. 14, No. 4, Winter 2003.

FESTINGER, L. (1957)

A Theory of Cognitive Dissonance. Evanston, IL: Row, Peterson and Company.

GHOSHAL, S. AND GRATTON, L. (2002)

'Integrating the enterprise'. *MIT Sloan Management Review*. Vol. 44, No. 1, Fall 2002.

GOLD, M. (1999)

The Complete Social Scientist: a Kurt Lewin reader. Washington, DC: American Psychological Association.

HANDY, C. (1989)

The Age of Unreason: new thinking for a new world. London: Random House Business Books.

HERON, J. (2001)

Helping the Client: a creative practical guide. 5th ed. London: Sage Publications.

HERZBERG, F., MAUSNER, B. AND SNYDERMAN, B. (1959)

The Motivation to Work. New York: John Wiley & Sons.

HIGGS, M. AND ROWLAND, D. (2003)

Is Change Changing? An examination of approaches to change and its leadership. Working Paper 0313, Henley Management College.

HONEY, P. AND MUMFORD, A. (1992)

Manual of Learning Styles. 3rd ed. Peter Honey Publications.

HONEY, P. AND MUMFORD, A. (2000)

Learning Styles Questionnaire. Peter Honey Publications.

HUYSMAN, M. (1999)

'Balancing biases: a critical review of the literature on organizational learning'. In: *Organizational Learning and the Learning Organization: developments in theory and practice.* Easterby-Smith, M., Araujo, L. and Burgoyne, J. (eds). London: Sage Publications.

ISAACS, W. (1999)

Dialogue and the Art of Thinking Together. Doubleday, New York.

JANIS, I.L. (1984)

'Groupthink'. In: Kolb, D.A., Rubin, I.M. and Mcintyre, J.M. (eds) *Organisational Psychology.* 4th ed. Englewood Cliffs, NJ: Prentice-Hall, Inc.

KAPLAN, R.S. AND NORTON, D.P. (1996)

The Balanced Scorecard: translating strategy into action. Boston: Harvard Business School Press.

KOLB, D.A. (1984)

Experiential Learning: experience as the source of learning and development. Englewood Cliffs, NJ: Prentice-Hall.

KOTTER, J.P. (1996)

Leading Change. Boston: Harvard Business School Press.

KOTTER, J.P. AND HESKETT, J.L. (1992)

Corporate Culture and Performance. New York: The Free Press.

LAVE, J. AND WENGER, E (1991)

Situated Learning: legitimate peripheral participation. Cambridge: Cambridge University Press.

LEARNING DECLARATION GROUP (2000)

A Declaration on Learning – Version 2. Atwood, M., Boydell, T., Burgoyne, J., Clutterbuck, D., Cunningham, I., Garratt, R., Honey, P., Mayo, A., Megginson, D., Mumford, A., Pearn, M., Pedler, M. and Wood, R. (Eds.). Visit: www.peterhoney.com/main/declaration.

LEWIN, K. (1947)

'Frontiers in group dynamics: concept, method and reality'. In: Social Science: Social Equilibrium and Social Change. *Human Relations.* Vol. 1, 5–41.

LIKERT, R. (1984)

'The nature of highly effective groups'. In: Kolb, D.A., Rubin, I.M. and McIntyre, J.M. (Eds.) *Organisational Psychology.* 4th ed. Englewood Cliffs, NJ: Prentice-Hall, Inc.

LITWIN, G.H. (1984)

'Climate and motivation: an experimental study'. In: Kolb, D.A., Rubin, I.M. and McIntyre, J.M. (Eds.) *Organisational Psychology.* 4th ed. Englewood Cliffs, NJ: Prentice-Hall, Inc.

LITWIN, G.H. AND STRINGER, R.A. (1968)

Motivation and Organisational Climate. Boston: Graduate School of Business Administration, Harvard University.

LIVINGSTON, J.S. (2003)

'Pygmalion in management'. *Harvard Business Review*, January 2003.

MARROW, A.J. (1969)

The Practical Theorist. New York: Basic Books, Inc.

MCGREGOR, D. (1966)

Leadership and Motivation: essays of Douglas McGregor. BENNIS, W.G. and SCHEIN, E.H. (eds). Cambridge, MA: The MIT Press.

O'REILLY, C.A. AND PFEFFER, J. (2000)

Hidden Value: how great companies achieve extraordinary results with ordinary people. Harvard Business School Press, Boston.

ORR, J. (1990)

'Sharing knowledge, celebrating identity: war stories and community memory in a service culture). In: Middleton, D.S. and Edwards, D. (eds), *Collective Remembering: memory in society.* Beverley Hills, CA: Sage Publications.

PAYNE, R. (2002)

'Organizations as psychological environments'. In: WARR, P. (ed.) *Psychology at Work.* London: Penguin Books.

PEDLER, M., BURGOYNE, J. AND BOYDELL, T. (1991)

The Learning Company: a strategy for sustainable development. London: McGraw-Hill.

ROTH, G. AND KLEINER, A. (2000)

Car Launch: the human side of managing change. London: Oxford University Press.

SATHE, V. AND DAVIDSON, E.J. (2000)

'Toward a new conceptualization of cultural change'. In: *Handbook of Organizational Culture and Climate.* ASHKANASY, N.M., WILDEROM, C.P.M. and PETERSON, M.F. Thousand Oaks, CA: Sage Publications, Inc.

SCHEIN, E.H. (1999)

The Corporate Culture Survival Guide: sense and nonsense about culture change. San Francisco: Jossey-Bass Publishers.

SCHULTZ, D.P. AND SCHULTZ, S.E. (1998)

Psychology and Work Today: an introduction to industrial and organizational psychology. New Jersey: Prentice-Hall, Inc.

SENGE, P.M. (1999)

'Learning for a change'. *Fast Company*, Issue 24, May 1999. Visit: http://www.fastcompany.com/online/24/senge.html.

SENGE, P.M., KLEINER, A., ROBERTS, C., ROSS, R. ROTH, G. AND SMITH, B. (1999)

The Dance of Change: the challenges of sustaining momentum in learning organizations. London: Nicholas Brealy Publishing.

SLOMAN, M. (2003)

Training in the Age of the Learner. London: Chartered Institute of Personnel and Development.

VYGOTSKY, L.S. (1962)

Thought and Language. Cambridge, MA: MIT Press.

VYGOTSKY, L.S. (1978)

Mind in Society: the development of higher psychological processes. Cambridge, MA: Harvard University Press.

WARR, P. (ED.) (2002)

Psychology at Work. London: Penguin Books.

WEICK, K.E. AND QUINN, R.E. (1999)

'Organizational change and development'. *Annual Review of Psychology.* 50: 361–86.

WENGER, E. (1998)

Communities of Practice: learning, meaning and identity. Cambridge: Cambridge University Press.